Photoshop 6.0

A *to* Z

The essential visual reference guide

Peter Bargh

Focal Press

OXFORD • AUCKLAND • BOSTON • JOHANNESBURG • MELBOURNE • NEW DELHI

Words and design: Peter Bargh
All photographs: Peter Bargh, unless stated
e-mail peter@bargh.co.uk

Focal Press
An imprint of Butterworth-Heinemann
Linacre House, Jordan Hill, Oxford OX2 8DP
225 Wildwood Avenue, Woburn, MA 01801-2041
A division of Reed Educational and Professional Publishing Ltd

A member of the Reed Elsevier plc group

First published 2001
© Peter Bargh 2001

British Library Cataloguing in Publication Data
A catalogue record for this book is available from the British Library

Library of Congress Cataloguing in Publication Data
A catalogue record for this book is available from the Library of Congress

ISBN 0 240 51655 9

Thanks to:
All at Focal Press (Oxford) for helping ensure Photoshop 5.5 A to Z was a success.
Elaine Swift at Nikon (Kingston-upon-Thames) for loaning me a Coolpix 950 camera.
Hendersons (Sheffield) for excellent relish.
Katie Teesdale (Boston) for her mighty fine chilli and weird milky drinks.
And finally, a specially thanks to everyone (World) who bought Photoshop 5.5 A to Z

This week I have mostly been listening to Mark Van Hoen (London).

Printed and bound in Italy by Printer Trento S.r.l.

PLANT A TREE

BTCV
British Trust for
Conservation Volunteers

FOR EVERY TITLE THAT WE PUBLISH, BUTTERWORTH-HEINEMANN
WILL PAY FOR BTCV TO PLANT AND CARE FOR A TREE.

Contents

Introduction

Photoshop is one of the most complex image editing programs sold, and many of the reference books are equally complex. *Photoshop 6.0 A to Z* has been produced to present the program in a visual way and in a logical order.

It's too easy to get lost wading your way around a 300 page book trying to find out how a certain feature works. In this book you look up the mode, tool or filter, presented in a logical A to Z order, to find a visual reference with handy tips and quick keys.

The book can be used as a helpful guide to keep near your computer, giving you nuggets of essential information as you work. It will also give you plenty of ideas to try on your own pictures.

It's really important when working with a program like Photoshop that you set it up to work better for you. To do this there are a selection of preferences that are used to take the program off the original settings and customise it to your liking. I've included an explanation of all these in the appendices, along with a comparison of all the versions of Photoshop.

As an English author I would naturally prefer to use English spellings, for example colour instead of color, but as the book will be sold throughout the world I've adopted the US spelling for the word color. This ensures the book is consistent with the Photoshop users' manual and interface.

I've also used Apple Mac commands throughout the book along with Mac screengrabs, simply because I've used a Mac for years in favour of the PC. Essentially Photoshop runs the same whichever platform you work on. The main difference is when a keyboard shortcut includes the Command key on a Mac you would use the Ctrl key on a PC. Similarly when the Option key is used on a Mac the Alt key should be used on the PC, and the Return key on the Mac is Enter on the PC. Enjoy!

Pete Bargh

Peter Bargh, 2001

Actions

MENU   WINDOW →
              SHOW ACTIONS

QUICK KEY F9

An action is a way of automatically applying a technique to an image using a pre-recorded series of commands, or a script, that is triggered by pressing

ACTIONS PALETTE
You can turn part of an action on or off, as well as record, play or edit new or existing actions.

one or a combination of keys. Many actions are already supplied with Photoshop and may be as simple as opening a new canvas or as advanced as creating a drop shadow on an existing picture or, as our example, making snow.

You can also create your own Photoshop actions using the Automate mode, so if there are techniques you find particularly fiddly or ones you'll want to use again, record the commands as you run through them and assign the action a shortcut key.

To record a new action open an image and select New Action from the hidden menu or click on the page icon at the bottom of the palette. This displays a new palette. Name your action, choose a destination folder, a shortcut key and a color for the button display.

The shortcut can be a single F button or any combination of an F along with Shift and Control keys. Click on the record button and run through the various steps to produce the desired result. You'll see each step appear in the menu as it's recorded. When you've done click stop.

Now whenever you want to apply the recorded effect just click on the designated shortcut key. Actions can also be applied to several images in one go using the Batch command. **(See Batch command and Droplets)**

Tips

● If a command cannot be recorded you can insert it manually using the Insert Menu command.
● If you make a mistake, keep going, you can edit the script later.
● Some settings may need modifying for different images. Clicking on the box to the left of the action will stop the script at that point and bring up the dialogue box so you can manually adjust before continuing the script.

Active Layer

This is the layer that is currently selected. To select a layer click on the layer icon in the layers palette. The layer will become highlighted and when a filter effect or brush is applied it will only affect the highlighted layer.

Adjustment Layer

MENU   LAYER ➜ NEW ADJUSTMENT LAYER   An adjustment layer is a layer that you can apply effects to that will change all the layers below it in the stack. If you then turn off the eye icon next to the layer it will turn off the effects for that particular adjustment layer. It's great for hand coloring black & white pictures as well as controlling levels or curves. You can delete these layers at any time to remove the effect.

As you select areas save them as Adjustment layers. You can then adjust the color of just the selection without affecting the rest of the picture, as illustrated here.

Airbrush

QUICK KEY J SELECTS IT FROM TOOLBOX   A painting tool that applies a color in much the same way as a real airbrush.

Hold down the mouse and drag it around to spray the color evenly onto the canvas. Hold it in the same place and the color builds up and spreads outwards. Covering an area that's already sprayed builds up color.

As with all brush modes you can specify size, blending mode and opacity using the bar that appears at the top of the page when you click on a brush tool.

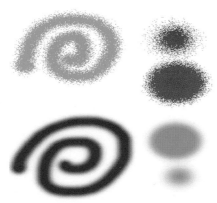

You could go wild with the color and if you don't like it (I can't think why!) you can revert to the original by either dumping the Adjustment layers or re-adjusting the color settings.

A Curves Adjustment layer was used to color our black & white original. It isn't bad and with practice you can obtain life-like results.

Tips
● Select a start point, hold down the Shift key and click an end point to paint a straight line.
● Use the Airbrush on low pressure with black paint to create shadows.
● Switch on Caps lock to turn the Airbrush standard cursor into a precision crosshair.

Tip
● In Version 5.5 open from Layer➜New➜Adjustment Layer.

Alpha channels

Are ideal for saving selections separate from the RGB or CMYK channels. Carefully draw round a subject and chose Select→Save Selection once you're happy with the selection. This is then stored at the bottom of the

Channels palette as a separate channel, known as the Alpha channel.

It can be recalled and the selection applied to the image at any time by calling up Load Selection from the Select menu. This saves you having to reselect a subject later. Up to 21 Alpha channels can be added to an RGB image allowing you to produce very complex selections that can be recalled to make changes to a variety of detailed parts of the image at any time.

Alpha channels can also be used to store fifth color info for special printing jobs.
(See Channels)

Tip
● Alpha channels can be combined to add selections together.

Anchor points

QUICK KEY J SELECTS IT
FROM TOOLBOX

The small square boxes that are placed around an object when you make a selection with the Pen tool. The points can be moved when they've been placed using the Direct Selection tool.

Pixels can make smooth edges look jagged.

Anti-aliasing

Aliasing occurs when the sharp edges of pixels appear jagged on the straight edges of an image or text.

Photoshop uses anti-aliasing to smooth out the edges by making the pixels semi-transparent so that they pick up color from surrounding pixels. It's useful when cutting or copying and pasting selections onto new backgrounds. Anti-aliasing can make the image look a little blurred when viewed close up.

Artifacts

Digital photography, like any form of image capture, can produce faults. In digital photography they're referred to as artifacts and can be caused by a number of problems including flare from the camera's lens, electrical interference or low resolution CCDs. Low resolution CCDs cause curved edges to appear jagged as the curve takes on the square edges of each pixel – known as Aliasing.

Blooming is less of a problem now but occurred on earlier CCDs when the electrical charge exceeded the pixel's storage capacity and crossed into adjacent pixels causing image distortion. We've all seen the TV presenter with the stripy shirt appearing as a strange colored pattern. The same thing happens on CCDs and it's known as color fringing.

Apply image

MENU   **IMAGE➔**   Used to blend one image layer and
          APPLY IMAGE   channel with another. The source and
destination image have to be the same size. I found the effect
works well using the same image with the blend option. It's
very much a trial and error process but well worth the effort as
seen here as I've appeared to change the season in one
simple step. **(See Calculations)**

A winter day made possible by the Lighten Blend mode and blue channel.

A hand coloured feel by blending the blue channel in Lighten mode.

A stormy summer day using Subtract blending mode and the blue channel.

Brush: 21   Mode: Normal   Opacity: 100%   Style: Tight Short   Fidelity: 100%   Area: 50 px   Spacing: 0%

Art History Brush

QUICK KEYS **SHIFT+Y ALTERNATES**
BETWEEN HISTORY AND
ART HISTORY BRUSHES

History Brush Tool
Art History Brush

A feature introduced in version 5.5 that will appeal to artists as, with a little experimentation, it can create some stunning painterly effects.

You choose from a variety of patterns and select the Blending mode and opacity before painting over an existing image. The more you paint over the same area the greater the effect. The larger the brush size the bigger the paint daubs and less realistic the effect.

Colorful images like this are suitable for the Art History Brush attack.

With a small brush and careful choice of the palette options paint effects can be quite realistic (left).

Choose too large a brush size and the effect could go completely wrong (far left).You could use this sort of treatment as background to text, though.

Art History Brush
(cont).

Although this isn't a particularly stunning example (I never said I was a painter!) it shows you can get depth by painting over larger brush strokes.

Try filling the picture with a color (black in this example) and paint from the previous history state on the colored fill.

Setting Fidelity to a low value produces brush strokes that have more color than the source point (left). A high value maintains the source color (right).

Tip

● Using one of the other custom brushes from Photoshop's Goodies folder will produce more unusual results.
 Here the cross brush was used to give a pastel/starburst effect.

Artistic filters

MENU   FILTER →   Change your picture into a painterly image
     ARTISTIC →   using this batch of filters that mimics natural or traditional artists' effects.

DRY BRUSH
Paints edges using a dry brush technique that appears midway between an oil and watercolor effect. The range of colors is simplified as the filter looks at nearby pixels and blends them into areas of common color.
Brush Size: 9, Brush Detail: 10, Texture: 2

COLORED PENCIL
Produces a rough crosshatch effect by drawing over the original using colored pencils. Edges are retained and the original background image shows through the pencil strokes.
Pencil Width: 2, Stroke Pressure: 4,
Paper Brightness: 25, Fade filter 70%

CUTOUT
Builds up the image as though it's created by a collage of several pieces of torn colored paper. It has a similar look to a posterization effect.
Number of levels: 8, Edge Simplicity: 5,
Edge Fidelity: 3

NEON GLOW
Adds a glow to parts of the image. The glow color is selected by clicking the glow box and choosing a color from the color picker.
Size: -1, Brightness: 30, Color: Blue, Fade filter 81% with Luminosity Blend mode

FILM GRAIN
Applies a pattern of grain that simulates real film. The higher you set the grain the more like fast film the effect becomes.
Grain: 7, Highlight Area: 7, Intensity: 2

FRESCO
Converts the image into a coarse stippled effect using short, rounded, and quickly applied brush dabs. Good for a Classic painting effect.
Brush Size: 0, Brush Detail: 7, Texture: 3,
Fade filter by 55%

ROUGH PASTELS
Makes an image appear as though it's on a textured background, covered in colored pastel chalk strokes. Chalk appears thick with little texture in bright colored areas and thinly sketched in darker areas.
Stroke Length: 39, Stroke Detail: 2,
Texture: Canvas, Scaling: 60%, Relief: 49,
Light Direction: Top

PAINT DAUBS
A nice effect varied by altering the brush size to between 1 and 50, with a selected brush type that includes simple, light rough, light dark, wide sharp, wide blurry and sparkle.
Size: 21, Sharpness: 45, Brush Type: Simple

PALETTE KNIFE
Similar to cutout, but with more blurred edges to emulate a palette knife style of painting. Will only suit certain images.
Stroke Size: 12, Stroke Detail: 3, Softness: 2

PLASTIC WRAP
Create Terminator style morphing by coating the image with a shiny plastic effect that accentuates surface detail.
Highlight Strength: 16, Detail: 3, Smoothness: 15

SMUDGE STICK
Uses diagonal strokes to smudge or smear the darker areas and soften the image while lighter areas become brighter and lose detail.
Stroke Length: 8, Highlight Area: 17, Intensity: 3

SPONGE
This is supposed to give an appearance of the image being painted with a sponge. Hmmm!
Brush Size: 0, Definition: 8, Smoothness: 15, Fade filter 68% with Luminosity Blend mode

UNDERPAINTING
Makes the image appear with a textured background that shows through the surface.
Brush Size: 0, Texture Coverage: 30, Texture: Stone, Scaling: 141%, Relief: 8, Light Direction: Top right

POSTER EDGES
Creates poster style effects by reducing the number of colors in the image and adding black lines around edges.
Edge Thickness: 6, Edge Intensity: 8, Posterization: 6

WATERCOLOR
Saturates colors and paints in a watercolor style by simplifying image detail. Can become too contrasty if you're not careful.
Brush Detail: 9, Shadow Intensity: 0, Texture: 2

Assign profile

MENU   **IMAGE →**

MODE →

ASSIGN PROFILE

An option that lets you select a colour profile to your image so that it will always request being opened in this mode or will indicate that a different profile is being used.

Audio Annotation tool

If you have a microphone plugged into the audio-in point of your computer you can record short audio messages and place them on a picture. The annotation appears as a small speaker icon which, when clicked, will replay the recording. This is a great tool for designers who want to leave messages to the next person who will work on the image. It's also open to abuse!
(See Note)

Auto Contrast

MENU **IMAGE →**

ADJUST →

AUTO CONTRAST

Auto mode that looks at the brightest and darkest parts of the image and adjusts the picture's highlights and shadows. It works well on some images, but it's often better to adjust the picture using Levels or Curves.
(See Levels)

BEFORE

AFTER

Auto Levels

MENU **IMAGE →**

ADJUST →

AUTO LEVELS

Scanned images using the auto setting rarely turn out with correct color or density so you need to adjust brightness and contrast.

Auto Levels looks for the brightest and darkest points and adjusts contrast so both maintain detail. It's a quick and easy fix, but learning how to adjust Levels manually produces better results.
(See Levels)

BEFORE

AFTER

Automate

MENU **FILE →**

AUTOMATE

A series of pre-written auto tasks used to make contact sheets, multi-format prints, batch conversions and format pictures for your Web page.

b

a**b**cdefghijklmnopqrstuvwxyz

Background color
Background Eraser
Batch processing
Bevels
Bézier curves
Bicubic interpolation
Bitmap images
Bitmap mode
Blending modes
Blur filters
Borders
Brightness
Brush creating
Brush editing
Brush size
Burn tool
Button mode

Background color

QUICK KEYS X ALTERNATES BETWEEN BACKGROUND AND FOREGROUND COLOR The default is white which appears in the lower box of the tools palette. You can change the color from white by clicking on this box and using the color picker to select a new one. One reason for doing this is when making gradient fills which progress from the foreground to background color. Erasing part of an image leaves the background color.
(See Foreground color)

Tip

● To fill a selection with the Background color press Command Delete.

Background Eraser

A feature introduced on version 5.5 that makes selections even easier. Rub over the area you don't want and the Eraser makes it transparent. Then when you copy and paste to a new layer it will look more natural.

Discontiguous erases the sample color wherever it appears in the picture. Contiguous erases pixels that are connected and Find Edges preserves edge sharpness.

Tip

● Change the tolerance level when working on different areas of the image. A higher percentage can be selected when there's a definite variation between the edge of the selection.

Batch processing

MENU FILE →
AUTOMATE)
BATCH

If you've ever had to deal with a pile of images that all needed converting from one format to another or one color mode to another you'll welcome this feature with open arms. Batch processing takes a selection of images from a folder and performs action sequences that you've pre-recorded in the Actions palette. You can specify whether you want the processed files to replace the existing ones or create new versions in a different destination folder. **(See Actions)**

Bevels

MENU LAYER →
EFFECTS →
BEVEL & EMBOSS

A mode that produces stylish type that will leap off your page. It can also be used on colored shapes to create 3D panels and buttons.

Using the Effects palette you can adjust the highlight and shadow of the bevel to create shallow or deep 3D effects.

Results vary depending on the resolution of your image so experiment with the settings to find a suitable effect. Turn Apply on so you can see the changes as you play. To get you started here are several I made using a 7x3cm canvas with a resolution of 300ppi and 50 point text.

Just a few examples of some of the effects you can obtain using Bevel effects.

Bevels & emboss settings explained

DEPTH
Determines how wide the highlight and shadow detail is. This can be varied between one and 20 pixels.

TECHNIQUE
Method of style set. Smooth is good for all types of bevels while Chisel is better for text.

STYLE
Lets you choose from four bevel options including Outer and Inner bevels, Emboss and Pillow Emboss.

UP/DOWN
When checked Up puts the shadow at the top of the text. Down puts it at the bottom.

SOFTEN
Goes from 0 with a very sharp highlight and shadow detail to 50 which is extremely soft. Numbers below 5 tend to offer a better bevel.

SIZE
Controls the size or amount of the bevel.

ANGLE
Click on this and move the mouse to adjust the angle that the highlight and shadow appear on the text.

GLOSS CONTOUR
Creates a glossy, metal style effect that can be varied by selecting from the range of graphs .

USE GLOBAL LIGHT
Sets the preferred angle for the lighting effects when you then select Use Global Angle from within the Layers option palette.

ALTITUDE
Controls the depth of shading. 90° gives a flat result that loses the bevel. As you go closer to 0° the bevel effect becomes more pronounced.

MODE
Determines how the color of the highlight and shadow will blend with the text color.

OPACITY
Varies the strength of effect that the highlight and shadow will produce on the text.

COLOR
You can choose the color of the highlight and shadow.

Bézier curves (bay-zee-ay)

Curves created using Photoshop's Pen tool are called Bézier curves, named after French mathematician Pierre Bézier.

The shape of a curve is created by the position of anchor points and direction lines that can be moved to change its shape and direction. They're used to make perfect selections around smooth or curved objects.

Bicubic interpolation

Used to increase the image size by adding pixels based on the average of the colors of all eight surrounding pixels. It also boosts contrast between pixels to avoid a blurring effect that's usually evident from interpolation. It's the slowest of the three interpolation processes, but it's the most precise and gives the smoothest gradation between tones. **(See Interpolation)**

Tip

● To ensure Bicubic is selected as a default go to File→Preferences →General and pull the option down in the interpolation box drop down menu.

Bitmap images

An image made up of a grid of squares (pixels) also known as a Raster image and not to be confused with Bitmap mode.

Bitmap images are resolution-dependent which means the number of pixels used to make up the image is fixed.

A bitmap is good at reproducing subtle colors, but jagged effects can occur when the image is enlarged.

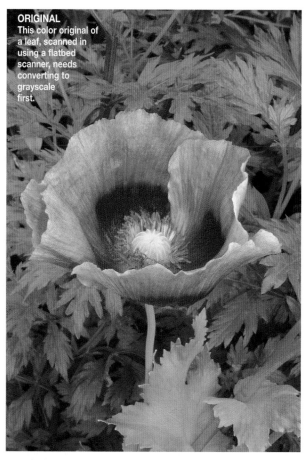

ORIGINAL
This color original of a leaf, scanned in using a flatbed scanner, needs converting to grayscale first.

Bitmap mode

MENU   IMAGE →   Converts the picture
ADJUST →   into a grid of black &
BITMAP   white pixels. The
option won't be available if you're trying to convert a color image. Discard color first by selecting Image→Mode→ Grayscale. Set output in the dialogue box to your inkjet printer's resolution.

GRAYSCALE
The color image converted to grayscale using Image|Mode|Grayscale.

50% THRESHOLD
Pixels with grey values above mid-grey convert to white and the rest become black resulting in a very high contrast, black & white image.

PATTERN DITHER
Converts the image into a geometric pattern of black & white dots that produce a range of grays when viewed.

DIFFUSION DITHER
Produces a film-like grain that's useful for viewing images on a black & white monitor.

HALFTONE SCREEN
Converts a grayscale image to simulate a printer's halftone dots.

CUSTOM PATTERN
First define your own pattern and then apply this pattern as a texture screen.

Blending modes

A range of modes selected from within the Options or Layers palettes. The modes control how the pixels in the base image are affected by a Brush, Editing tool or other Layer.

Here's what happens when a photograph of the moon is placed on a new layer and blended with a sky.

COLOR
Produces an end color with the luminance of the base color and the hue and saturation of the blend color. It's a good mode for hand-coloring black & white images as it keeps the gray tones.

DISSOLVE
When two layers are combined there's no effect unless the active layer has been feathered and then a splattering effect appears in the feathered area to produce the dissolved colors.

NORMAL
The default mode, which appears as Threshold when you're working with bitmap or indexed color images. When the layer or brush is set at 100% the pixels produce the end color and are not affected by the base image. Change the opacity and the colors blend and form an average.

HARD LIGHT
Adds color together and, like Soft Light, lightens image areas lighter than 50% grey and darkens the Blend color if it's already darker than 50% gray. Painting with black or white produces pure black or white. A Harsh overlay.

COLOR BURN
Merges the darker colors of the upper layer or paint with the base layer. Blending with white has no effect on the overall image.

COLOR DODGE
Uses the upper layer or paint to add color and brighten the color of the base layer. Blending with black doesn't affect the image.

DARKEN
Looks at the color in each layer and selects the darker of the base or blend layer as the final color. Lighter pixels are replaced, darker pixels stay the same.

EXCLUSION
A similar, but lower contrast effect to the Difference mode.

HUE
Produces a combined color that includes the luminance and saturation of the base color and the hue of the blend color.

LIGHTEN
Looks at the color in each layer and selects the lighter of the base or blend layer as the final color. Pixels darker than the blend color are replaced and lighter pixels stay the same.

b

LUMINOSITY
Mixes hue and saturation of the base color and the luminance of the blend color and creates the opposite effect of Color mode.

SATURATION
Takes the hue and luminance of the base color and blends it with the saturation of the applied color.

MULTIPLY
Painting over the base color with the blend color produces a darker color. Painting with black changes the base color to black, while white leaves the color unchanged. Painting repeatedly over the same area produces progressively darker colors and is similar to coloring with a felt tip pen. The active layer becomes darker when this mode is selected.

SCREEN
Opposite performance to Multiply with the end color always lighter. Painting with black leaves the color unchanged while white produces white. The active layer becomes lighter.

OVERLAY
Similar process to Multiply, but Overlay holds onto the base color's highlights and shadows while mixing with the active layer to produce an image with more contrast. Use this mode with a Paintbrush to build up a hand-coloring effect.

SOFT LIGHT
Similar to Overlay, but more subtle. If the blend color is lighter than 50% gray, the whole image will lighten. If it's darker than 50% gray, the image will darken. How much depends on the paint color used. When you merge layers you benefit from a lighter image.

Blur filters

A series of effects accessed from the filter pull down menu and used to soften all, or part, of an image by reducing the defined edges between pixels. Quite silly really – you have a camera that's been carefully engineered to give razor sharp images that

you're now going to make blurred! The beauty with a digital image is you can control how much and where the blur will occur. So consider having infinite control of depth-of-field or the ability to soften wrinkles and hide freckles while keeping the eyes sharp. Now you're thinking! There are six options in the Photoshop filter menu that include Blur, Blur More, Gaussian Blur, Motion Blur, Radial Blur and Smart Blur.

BLUR

Smoothes out color transitions in an image by averaging out pixels next to hard edges of defined lines and shaded areas. This is a good mode to help smooth out harsh looking pictures created using a digital camera.

Straight shot from an Olympus Camedia digital camera.

Blur filter applied.

Fade Blur filter applied to give a more subtle blur.

BLUR MORE

Similar effect to the Blur filter, but up to four times as strong. The transfers on the car door have been enlarged so you can see the effect of the blur that's been added.

Original taken with a Nikon Coolpix 950 digital camera.

Blur More filter applied.

Fade Blur More with Blend mode set to Exclusion gives solarization.

GAUSSIAN BLUR

An adjustable blurring effect, controlled by one slider that adjusts the pixel radius in 1/10 pixels from 0.1 to 250. It adds low-frequency detail that can produce a hazy effect.

The picture in the preview window can be adjusted in size so you can watch the result on a localized area or the whole picture. The preview appears quicker if the area is magnified.

MOTION BLUR

Recreates slow shutter speed effects by blurring adjacent pixels at user selectable angles through 360°. You can also control the intensity of the blur producing a streak with a length of between 1 and 999 pixels.

RADIAL BLUR

Recreate zoom lens or rotating blurring effects with this mode. Ticking the Spin box makes the image look as though it's, wait for it, spinning. You then specify a degree of rotation by dragging the slider across while viewing a graphical representation of the rotation.

Tick the Zoom box to blur along radial lines and produce the same effect as adjusting a camera's zoom lens during a long exposure. You can adjust the depth from 1 to 100 pixels. You also have the option of Draft for fast, but grainy results or Good and Best for smoother results. Unlike in-camera effects you can also move the centre point of the effect off-centre by dragging the pattern in the graphic preview box.

b

SMART BLUR

Smart Blur first appeared in Version 4 of Photoshop and leaves edges sharp while blurring lower contrast parts of the image, often resulting in a posterization or watercolor style effect.

Radius and Threshold sliders are provided to control the blurring effect by the depth of pixels affected and their values. There's also a quality box that has low, medium or high quality blur options. And a final box to set the filter to work on the entire selection in Normal mode, or for the edges of color transitions using Edge Only and Overlay.

Edge Only produces a graphic black & white edge effect while Overlay Edge blends the graphical edge effect with the original image.

A careful blend of all four can produce some very creative images, but can also be used to reduce film grain or blemishes without affecting the overall result.

Borders

MENU   SELECT ➜

MODIFY ➜

BORDER

It's easy to add a border to your whole image or a selection. With an area selected choose the Border command and enter a width in pixels.

The thickness of border is relative to the original image size – a 3 pixel border on a 300 pixel wide image will look twice as thin as one with 600 pixel width.

When applied you'll have a second set of dotted lines "marching ants" which you can fill using the Bucket tool or Edit➜Fill command. Choose the color border you want and set this as the foreground color before applying the fill.

Tips

● Turn off Preserve Transparency in the Layers palette to apply a Blur filter to the edges of a layer.
● Create pencil drawings by running the Smart Blur set to Edge Only mode (middle). Then Invert Image➜Adjust➜Invert to get a black sketch on white paper (right).

Tips

● Don't go mad! Black or neutral colors can look more striking than a vivid red or blue. You don't want all the attention on the border!
● Thin borders set a picture off – thick ones can be messy.
● Borders made using the Border mode always have a softer inner edge. To produce a sharp defined border use the Stroke command.
(See Stroke)

Brightness

MENU   **IMAGE** ➜
            ADJUST ➜
BRIGHTNESS/CONTRAST

Adjust the intensity of the image using this slider control. You can go from –100 to +100 which gives the equivalent of about three stops' exposure control that you'd experience using slide film. While this is a quick and easy option it's better to use Levels or Curves for more precise control.

Brush creating

A useful feature hidden away within Photoshop's brush edit menu is the Define Brush mode. Selecting part of any image, followed by Edit|Define Brush, will allow the selection to be used as a brush pattern. You can also create your own simple graphics and use them as a brush pattern.

Make a selection from a suitable area of an image. Then choose Define Brush and start to paint. Saturation mode was used to create the colorful canvas, above, which was then treated to Motion Blur to create the background image, below.

You can also use the pre-set range of brushes that need to be loaded from Photoshop's Goodies folder. Photoshop 6 has a range of new brushes that can be called up by clicking on the arrow to the right of the brush size icon and then on the arrow at the side of the palette that appears. From here you can also edit brushes or delete ones from the existing palette.

Brush editing

Photoshop 6.0 has changed the way we see brush options. In previous versions you double clicked on the Brush tool to open the options palette and from there you could select the brush size, opacity and blend mode. Now a convenient bar appears across the top as soon as you click on any tool. This makes it much quicker to edit, once of course you've become familiar with the new way of working. The 16 brushes that appear as standard in this bar can be edited and added to. Double clicking on one brings up an editing palette where you can

choose the diameter, hardness and spacing of the brush. You can also choose the angle and roundness.

The diameter is selected in pixel width and can be anything from 1 to 999 pixels wide. Hardness determines how sharp the edge of the brush is and ranges from 0% to 100% Spacing varies the gap between each shape when you paint and can be set between 1% and 999%. A setting of 100% produces a shape that touches edge to edge, 50% overlaps by half so every alternate shape touches and 150% leaves a gap half the width of a shape between each shape. Got the idea? The angle comes

To illustrate the effect of the Spacing feature I first created an oblique shaped brush and increased spacing in increments of 100% for each of the arrows I've drawn on the canvas.

into play when you've changed the roundness and is great for creating Calligraphy style brush strokes.

Brushes that have been created using Define pattern can only be edited using the Spacing control.

Brush size

MENU   WINDOW →
        SHOW BRUSHES
QUICK KEY F5

Varying the size of a paint brush is essential when working with different images. Where a large background may suit a chunky brush,

retouching a very small area would need a brush tip that may be just one pixel wide. This level of adjustment is made in the Brushes menu bar, which has a selection of pre-set sizes to choose from, but custom sizes can be also be created. It's not just paint brushes that benefit from size – you can also adjust the Eraser, Smudge, Dodge & Burn tools, and, in this example, the Clone tool which made it much quicker to duplicate the boat. Its color was then changed.

Burn tool

QUICK KEY   SHIFT+O A few of Photoshop's tools are based around the conventional photographer's aids and the Burn tool is one of them.

Drag this icon, that's shaped like a hand making an O shape, over the image to darken it – like you would in the darkroom using card with a hole cut out to let more light onto the paper.

You have a choice of how the Burn tool affects the image. Highlight darkens the light parts of the image, Midtones affects the mid-grays and Shadows adjusts the dark parts.

Toggle between the Burn, Dodge and Saturate icons using Shift+O. Use the opacity setting to vary the strength.

Button mode

A pretty looking interface that's an alternative to the normal Actions palette and is selected from the black triangle drop down menu. Each Action is assigned a color, making it easy to group similar Actions. This mode is useful for less experienced users of the Actions feature, but scripts can't be edited so more advanced users should stay clear. **(See Actions)**

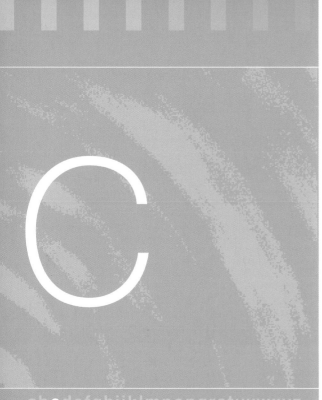

Calculations

MENU   IMAGE →
          CALCULATIONS

This mode lets you merge two channels from one or two images and save the result as a new channel in one of the existing images or create a new image. The Calculations palette gives you various options including Blend method and is useful if you want to combine masks or selections.

Calibration

The phrase 'what you see is what you get', or 'wysiwyg' (pronounced whizzywig) couldn't be more important. When you view an image on the computer screen you want it to appear exactly the same when it prints out – oh if life were so simple! Computer monitors can be wildly out – just like your neighbour's television, and a high contrast, vivid color image on screen is likely to be disappointingly dull when printed.

It's because the image on the monitor is an RGB file that's projected light, while the printed image is a CMYK version that you view by reflected light. To get round this you need to calibrate your system. Adjust the monitor using Adobe's Gamma file which should be located in your control panels directory. This easy-to-follow wizard guides you through adjusting brightness, contrast and gamma to help you get more life-like prints. It's also worth looking out for the scanner and printer profiles which ensure that the file keeps consistent color as it moves through your system.

Canvas size

The canvas is the base to your picture; like an artist would add paint to his, you add pixels to yours. When an image is opened the canvas size is the same as the image. If you want to extend to one side or to the top or bottom you need to increase the canvas size. Click on the square where you want your existing canvas to be extended from. Here I've illustrated how to increase the canvas from 5x4in to 7x5in. I clicked in the top right of the grid of nine squares so that the canvas extends along the bottom and right of the existing canvas.

Channels

MENU WINDOW →

SHOW CHANNELS

Each file in Photoshop is made up of channels that store information about the image. A freshly created RGB file has a channel for each of the three colors, and a CMYK has four channels, while Duotones and Index color images have just one.

You can add channels to store info about the picture. For example, Alpha channels can be added to save selections as masks. Then when you want to perform a similar cutout in the future you load the Alpha channel to bring the marching ants into play on the selected layer.

Channels can also be edited individually so you could blend certain ones, or fiddle with the color of just one channel – useful when you want to make a selection based on a certain color which would be easier to do in its own environment.

Tip

● Individual color channels appear as black & white. If you'd prefer to see them in color go to File→ Preferences→Displays & Cursors and select the Color Channels in Color option.

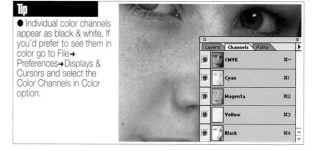

Channel Mixer

MENU   IMAGE →
ADJUST →
CHANNEL MIXER →

The Channel mixer is one of those tools in Photoshop that you come to once you have a little more experience. By adjusting the color of the individual R, G and B channels you can change the color of an element within the picture. In this example a simple adjustment of the red slider in the red channel was reduced from 100% to 0%.

The Channel mixer can also be accessed from the Adjustment Layer sub menu.

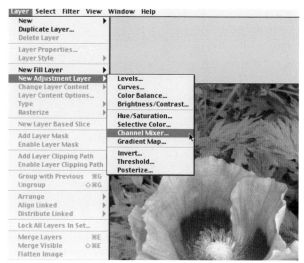

C

Channel Mixer
(cont.)

You could play around mixing channel colors all day! If you don't like the result, click on cancel and start again.

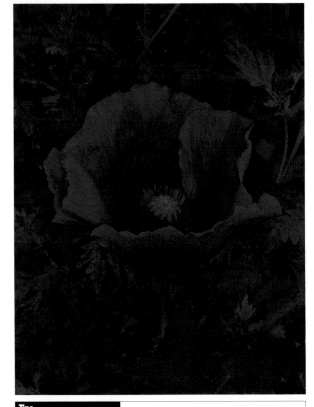

Clipping path

When an image is dropped into an illustration or desktop publishing page the background of the subject will appear on the page too. To avoid this draw around the subject that you want to bring into the design package and save the selection as a path.

When you've finished, save the file as an EPS which keeps all the clipping path data. Now when you place the saved

image on the page the background will appear transparent so you can flow text round the subject or drop it onto a different colored panel.

A clipping path was drawn around the swan so it can be dropped into a DTP layout without a background.

Clone Stamp tool

In Version 6.0 Adobe has followed most of the other software programs and given the oddly named Rubber Stamp tool a more sensible title of Clone Stamp tool. This particular tool is responsible for many photographers taking up digital imaging.

The first time you see bits of rubbish being wiped right out of an image or spots and blemishes being removed from your partner's face you'll be in awe. All that's happening is the Clone

Stamp tool is being used to pick up or sample pixels from one place and drop them somewhere else. It's one of the most used devices to remove or add detail to an image.

There are several ways to use it. For starters it acts like a brush so you can change the size, allowing cloning from just one pixel wide to hundreds. You can change the opacity to produce a subtle clone effect. You can select any one of the options from the Blend menu. And, most importantly, there's a choice between Clone align or Clone non-align.

To use it place the cursor over the sample point, hold down the Alt key and click the mouse. Then move the cursor to the point where you want the sample to appear and click the mouse to dump the pixels. If you hold down the mouse button and drag you'll paint from the sample area. Select Aligned from the Clone Stamp options palette and the sample cursor will follow the destination cursor around keeping the same distance away. When unaligned the sample cursor starts where you left off. Both choices have their advantages.

(See Pattern Stamp tool)

Scratches are fairly simple to remove. Keep a steady hand and follow patterns when Cloning.

Large objects are more difficult. Clone in the area roughly first and patch over the cloned area using other areas to create a more realistic effect.

Dust, caused by scanning an unclean transparency, can easily be removed. Just select areas of similar color or pattern from nearby and clone from those areas over the dust spot. Move in close and vary the size of the brush on different areas.

Whoops

● Avoid repetitive patterns caused by cloning the same area over and over again.

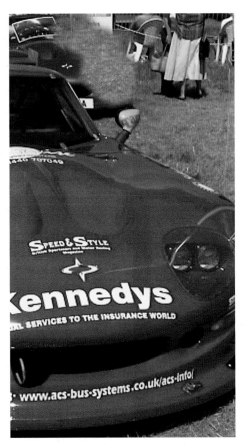

Some programs allow cloning to be applied at different percentages to produce a smaller or larger version of the original. Photoshop doesn't (right), but you can get round this by adding a new layer. Then take your sample point from the original layer and clone with the new layer active. Then use the Transform tool to rescale the cloned image (below).

Above: Clone aligned ensures the clone sample point stays at the same distance from the cursor as you move around cloning. This is useful when, for example, you're cleaning up blemishes or dust from a portrait. The sampling will always occur near to the cursor so the sampled pixels will usually be similar. In this example it's recloned the car I want to remove.

Clone unaligned keeps the sample point where you left off so when you move the cursor it stays put. This is useful when you want to take a certain part of the image and paint it in various other parts (right). Here I've taken the grass and begun to clone over the car using the same area repeatedly.

You can take your sample point from one image and then reposition the cursor on a different one to clone onto it.

Play God and create a new life. This started out with just four birds!

Clouds filter

MENU	FILTER →
	RENDER →
	CLOUDS

This useful addition to the Filters menu creates cloud effects that can be used as effective backgrounds to your pictures. Before selecting the filter make sure your background color is set to white and the foreground to the color sky you'd like. Blue creates natural skies while orange will deliver a sunset effect and black will produce a stormy sky.

Open a new canvas and set it to the size you want to end up with and select the filter. If you don't like the clouds that are created try again – it's random.

Draw around your subject to make a selection, then copy and paste the selection onto an image created using the Clouds filter. Try experimenting with colors for unusual effects.

CMYK

When a digital image is printed it's converted from RGB into CMYK. CMYK is the standard method of printing and uses Cyan, Magenta and Yellow inks to make up the various colors.

A 100% combination of C, M and Y should produce black, but in reality it's a murky brown color so the Black ink (K to avoid confusion with the Blue of RGB) ensures black is printed where necessary.

Tips

● If the cloud effect is too harsh make the original canvas smaller, apply clouds then increase its size.

● Go to Image→Adjust→Hue/Saturation (Ctrl+U), click on Colorize and adjust Hue to change color.

● Use the Gaussian or Motion Blur filter to soften the effect.

Collage

Strictly speaking a collage is a collection of photographs mounted together, but Photoshop creates a perfect alternative by bringing several photos together to form one larger image that hasn't seen a drop of glue or sticky tape.

It's a great technique to use to create a family tree, group photo, promo, surreal image or, as above, a panel to go on a Web site or stationery header and a record of a party (left).

Using Layers makes the job much easier and more controllable. Here Layer masks were used to create the various blends from one image to another. Blend modes and masks are used to allow lower layers to react with the ones above.

The binary text on the panel above was created using the text tool and then distorted, skewed and stretched to give it a forward look.

Color Balance

MENU	IMAGE →
	ADJUST →
	COLOR BALANCE
QUICK KEY	CTRL+B

Used to remove, or create a color cast. The Color Balance palette has three sliders to control the color.

Moving the top slider left adds cyan and reduces red. Move it to the right to add red and reduce cyan. The middle slider controls magenta and green and the bottom, yellow and blue. Precise values can be keyed in the top boxes. You can also select where you want the color to change, placing emphasis in the highlights, shadows or midtones. The final option is to Preserve Luminosity which maintains the original brightness when it's turned on.

(See Color Cast on page 26)

Color blend
(See Blending modes)

Color burn
(See Blending modes)

Color cast

Daylight film is designed to produce a natural looking range of colors for outdoor photography or indoor shots taken with flash.

Take a photo indoors without flash and you'll end up with a color cast. This will be green if the light source is fluorescent or orange if it's tungsten light.

Some flashguns are so harsh that they create a blue color cast. The walls in a room can also reflect light to add a color to your subject. Any color cast can be removed, or added, using Photoshop's Color Balance mode.

Color Channels
(See Channels)

Color dodge
(See Blending modes)

Color Range

**MENU   SELECT →
       COLOR RANGE**

Photoshop's Color Range is a versatile tool to help you select and change the color of a part of your picture. This could easily be a model's lipstick, car paint work or, as in this case, a red telephone box.

With the picture on a new layer go to call up the Color Range palette. To make it easier to see what you're doing click on Selection at the bottom of the palette to turn the preview window into a grayscale image. For this exercise also make sure Sampled Colors is in the Select menu item at the top of the palette.

Now click on the left-hand Eye-dropper tool and position your cursor over a part of the phone box and click once.

You'll see areas of white appear on the grayscale preview. These are red pixels that are similar in color to the red you've just clicked on.

The Fuzziness slider above the preview window controls the range of reds either side of the one you picked. Adjusting the slider to the right increases the selection, and to the left decreases the selection.

Tips

● Press CTRL to change the grayscale preview to the color image.

Color Range
(cont.)

Another method is to let Photoshop
pick the color you want to change.
Go to the Select menu and pull down
the Red option. Now you'll see the
Fuzziness scale cannot be adjusted
and everything that's red in the
image has been selected. You can
also use this method to select
highlights, midtones or shadows.

WHICH MASK?

The Color Range palette also lets you
choose which type of mask to put over
the image as you work. We've been
using None, but the menu box, labelled
Selection Preview at the bottom of the
palette, has four other options.

Grayscale makes the image look like the
palette's preview.

Black Matte makes the unselected area black.

White Matte makes the unselected area... you
guessed it, white.

Quick Mask puts red over unselected areas.

Color Sampler tool

An eyedropper tool that places up to four sample points on the photo so you can compare colour and density of each spot using the measurements displayed in the info palette.

Color Settings

MENU   EDIT ➜

COLOR SETTINGS

Allows you to set up color profiles so that images you open up use a pre-selected color space. Spend some time setting this up correctly and you'll maintain consistent color when the image is displayed and printed.

Colorize

(see next page)

Compression

Digital images can have huge file sizes. A 10x8in RGB image with a resolution of 300dpi, for example, has a file size of 21Mb. A few of these will start to fill up your computer's hard disk and a quick calculation finds you'll only even fit 30 on a CD. It doesn't have to be this way. There are several file formats that change the data to reduce the file size – a method known as compression.

Two types exist – Lossy and Lossless. Lossy removes data for good, Lossless keeps it all safe. JPEG is the common storage format used by most digital cameras and Kodak's Picture CD. JPEG is a Lossy version and can affect the picture quality if it's highly compressed.

Conditional mode change

MENU   FILE ➜

AUTOMATE ➜

CONDITIONAL

MODE CHANGE

Add this to an action to keep the color mode of a file the same when the action is being performed.

Contiguous
(See Magic wand)

Contact sheet

MENU   FILE ➜

AUTOMATE ➜

CONTACT SHEET

Photoshop has a neat conversion that takes a collection of images and turns them into low resolution thumbnails that are positioned like a contact sheet.

It's a good way of keeping a record of your images and also to submit with CDs so the client can have a rough visual of what's included in the package.

You can choose the size of sheet and the number of pictures displayed across the page.The quality is a bit disappointing, but it's quick and easy to use.

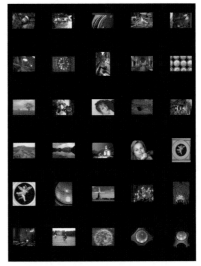

The pictures appear on the contact sheet in the same way that they have been saved. It's a shame you can't preview and rotate the pictures before you save the contact.

Tip
● The contact sheet is saved with a white background.
If you would prefer a different color use the Fill tool with a neutral tone selected for the paint and click on the transparent area to deposit the color of your choice.
Red might clash! Black's a safe choice.

Colorize

MENU **IMAGE** →
      ADJUST →
      HUE/SATURATION

Turned on in the Hue/Saturation palette to create a monocolor image. If you want to tone a black & white image first convert it to RGB, Image→Mode→RGB Color. Adjust the Hue slider and watch the image go from blue through the colors of the rainbow and back to blue. Stop when the image is the color you like and save. Use lightness and saturation sliders to vary color further.

Hue: 260, Saturation: 35

Original

Hue: 88, Saturation: 39

Hue: 36, Saturation: 29

Hue: 200, Saturation: 50

Hue: 0, Saturation: 33

Hue: 16, Saturation: 76, Lightness: −11

Hue: 133, Saturation: 53

Hue: 56, Saturation: 69, Lightness: −20

Hue: 310, Saturation: 46

Hue: 0, Saturation: 73, Lightness: 15

C

Contrast

MENU   IMAGE ➜
ADJUST ➜
BRIGHTNESS/
CONTRAST

The range of tones between black and white, or highlight and shadow.

A high contrast image is one where there's black and white, but not much in between. Shots taken into the sun, or with the sun high in the sky are often high contrast.

A low contrast image is one that doesn't have many tones in the lightest or darkest areas so it looks quite grey and flat. Pictures taken in mist or dull conditions are often low contrast. In the traditional darkroom contrast is controlled using special variable-contrast paper – in the digital lab you just adjust the sliders and watch the preview.

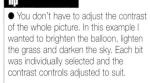

● You don't have to adjust the contrast of the whole picture. In this example I wanted to brighten the balloon, lighten the grass and darken the sky. Each bit was individually selected and the contrast controls adjusted to suit.

Brightness/Contrast

Brightness: +13   OK

Contrast: +75   Cancel
☒ Preview

Adjusting contrast in a color image makes colors look dull and subdued when contrast is decreased (left) or vivid when contrast is increased (right). Edges can become overly enhanced so the result looks very digital.

C

Convert to profile

MENU   **IMAGE →**
       MODE →
       CONVERT TO PROFILE

This has changed from its previous title of Profile to Profile in version 5.5. It lets you convert a picture into a different color space so you can ensure a more accurate result when viewing or printing.

Cursor

The cursor is where all the action is. It's the point of the brush, the insertion point, the Cloning source, etc. and is controlled by the mouse or keyboard arrows.

The way it appears can be changed by going to File→ Preference→Displays & Cursors.

Paint cursors can be set to Standard, Precise or Brush Size. The brush or tool icon appears when the cursor is set to Standard, a cross hair appears on Precise and a shape the size of the brush being used appears with Brush size. Which you use is a matter of personal preference and may vary depending on the work you're doing. Try all three in different circumstances and pick whichever works best.

Tip
- The standard curser shows an icon of the tool you are using. It's much better if you change to the presision or brush size icons.
(see Appendix D)

Crop tool

Use this to be more creative with your composition and cut out wasteful surrounds. Click and hold down the mouse to draw a frame around the subject. Then use the handles to resize or reposition. When you've included everything you want click in the centre to make anything outside the frame disappear.

Photoshop 6.0 has a new version of the crop tool that masks all the area surrounding the crop frame in a color and opacity of your choice. It's factory set at 75% black which gives a useful grey mask. This is much clearer to work with than previous versions and gives you a far better indication of the effect the crop will have on the image.

A tighter crop on this shot adds emphasis to the car. The new Crop tool in version 6 darkens the surrounding area to make it easier to judge the crop.

You can also click on perspective to allow the crop box to be adjusted to straighten out perspective problems or an off-vertical scanned image.

Curves

MENU	IMAGE →	The Curves
	ADJUST →	palette has
	CURVES	a graph with
QUICK KEY	CTRL+M	vertical and

horizontal scales representing input and output brightness. When you first open this you'll see a straight line running through the graph at 45° from the bottom left to the top right.

The bottom left represents the shadow area, top right is highlights and the mid-point is midtones. You can drag the line by clicking on it and holding down as you move the mouse. Moving the mid-point up also has a lightening effect and down to darken. These actions can be reversed by clicking on the little arrow on the brightness bar below the graph. Use the Eye-dropper tool and Ctrl+click anywhere on the image and its brightness value will appear as a point on the line. You can then move this point up or down to darken or lighten that part of the image. The picture will look natural, providing you create either a straight line or an arc.

Dragging the bottom left upwards lightens it.

Tips

● If you know what shape curve you want, select the Pen icon and draw the line in the box. This can be quicker than dragging the line around.

● Hold down the Alt key and click on the grid to make it finer.

C

Curves
(cont.)

Dragging the top right downwards darkens the picture.

Input: 255
Output: 193

Tip

● Create bizarre effects by saving a gradient as a Map Setting and then load that as a Curve. Double click on the Gradient tool. Then click on Edit in the Gradient tool palette. Select a bright gradient such as Rainbow and hold the Ctrl key down while clicking on the Save button. This will create a Map Setting file (*.AMP).

Go back to the Curves palette and click Load. From Files of Type: select the Map Setting option and locate the gradient that you've saved. Your picture will burst into a rainbow of colors.

Better black & white

● The Curves feature can be used to enhance your black & white pictures with ease. Simply open up the picture and the Curves palette. Click on the left-hand Eye-dropper tool and, using your mouse cursor, place the Eye-dropper icon on the darkest part of the image and click. Do the same with the right-hand Eye-dropper on the brightest area and click to produce an image with a more satisfactory tonal range.

You can also select up to 15 points on the line and pull them in either direction to create snake patterns and very interesting results. This is a mode to experiment with, especially if you enjoy creating surreal effects. If you stumble across a style you like you can save it to reuse on other images at a later date.

Custom color table

Images produced to be used on the Web need small file sizes. Photoshop reduces the number of colors from millions down to just 256 when it saves files as GIFs and the colors that are used can be saved as a custom table.

Custom Shape tool

Custom Shapes are selected from the tool bar with a variety of new shapes with Version 6.0. When selected they allow you to draw vector shapes that have editable path outlines. They can also be resized without any loss in definition as they are resolution independant.

Shapes can be filled with colors, patterns or images.

The Arrow Custom shape was selected and its path made into a selection. Then the selection was feathered and the car pasted into the selection – Edit→Paste Into. This creates a new layer with a layer mask that can then be edited.

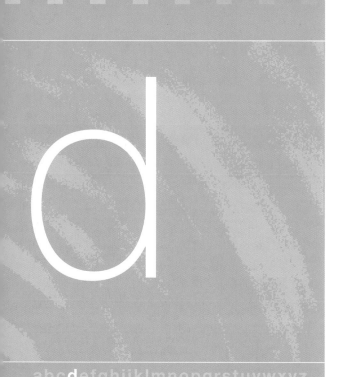

De-interlace filter

A filter used to smooth moving images captured on video.

Defringe

MENU   LAYER →   No matter how hard you try, when cutting
        MATTING →   round a subject you usually leave a few
        DEFRINGE   pixels from the old background. When you
paste the cutout to the new background the unwanted pixels
may stick out like a sore thumb. This yellow flower, for
example, cut out from a green background has a few green
pixels around the edge that show up when it's pasted to its
new red background.

   The Defringe command changes these green pixels to yellow
to produce a cleaner effect. Like most commands, you can
enter a pixel value, in this case, a width of between one and
64 pixels, depending on the nature of your original selection.

Desaturation

MENU	IMAGE →
	ADJUST →
	DESATURATE
QUICK KEY	SHIFT+CTRL+U

This mode takes all the color out of an RGB image, changing it to black & white without you having to convert it to grayscale. You can also produce this by dragging the Saturation slider to the left in the Hue/Saturation mode.

Distortion filter

| MENU | FILTER → |
| | DISTORT |

A collection of filters that distort the image. If you have an older computer be patient, some of these filters are memory intensive and apply to your image at a snail's pace.

DIFFUSE GLOW
Creates an effect similar to looking through a soft diffusion filter by adding see-through white noise to the image and a glow, fading from the centre of the selection. Can be used to simulate infrared film effects.The palette has sliders to control the graininess, amount of glow and clear amount.

Despeckle filter
(See Noise filter)

Deselect

MENU	SELECT →
	DESELECT
QUICK KEY	SHIFT+D

Removes 'marching ants' selection from the image.

Difference mode
(See Blending modes)

Dissolve mode
(See Blending modes)

Direct selection tool

QUICK KEYS SHIFT+A This is used to pick up Anchor points on a Path made by the Pen tool and either move the entire path, change a point or create a bézier curve around the subject.

d

DISPLACE

Changes the image into a pattern that's previously been saved as a Displacement Map. These can be created from your own images or you can use one of the 12 supplied in the Displacement Maps folder within Photoshop's Plug-Ins folder. These include Tiles, Streaks and Honeycomb.

The palette has options to tile a Displacement Map that's too small for the image you're applying it to or stretch it to fit. A tiled Map is the same image repeated to fit to the edges. The stretched version creates interesting effects and can be varied by changing the percentages in the horizontal and vertical scales.

GLASS

Applies a distorted effect that looks like the view through a bathroom window. There's a choice of four styles and others can be created and loaded manually.

The palette has sliders to control the distortion level, smoothness and scale which can then be viewed in the preview window.

POLAR COORDINATES

Unusual effect with two options to convert the image from either rectangular to polar coordinates or vice versa. Can be used with text to stretch it round an image, or combined with a few other filters to create strange backgrounds.

RIPPLE

Another effect like Ocean Ripple that creates a water pattern on the selected area.

The slider controls the amount of ripple and a pull down menu has three ripple sizes.

OCEAN RIPPLE
Similar effect to the Glass filter, offering two sliders to control ripple size and magnitude.

PINCH
A slider that varies from –100 to +100 to make the centre of the image appear to expand like a balloon or squeeze in like an hour glass.

SHEAR
Displays a grid and a straight vertical line that you pull around to make a curved shape. This shape transfers to the selected image, distorting it along the curve.

SPHERIZE
In Normal mode it produces a similar effect to Pinch. In Horizontal Only the image becomes thinner or thicker as you adjust the slider and in Vertical Only it becomes shorter or taller.

WAVE

An advanced version of the Ripple filter with seven sliders and five buttons to choose from that control the number of wave generators, the distance between waves, the height and the type. Experiment at your leisure or press the Randomize button and let it choose a value.

TWIRL

Creates a spiral effect similar to the way water goes down a plug hole. It works in a clockwise or anti-clockwise direction depending on where the slider is set.

ZIGZAG

Another Ripple style distortion but one that includes the realistic Pond Ripple option. Apply this to water and it will look just like you've thrown a pebble in before taking the photograph.

Document Size

Click on the small arrow in the bottom left-hand corner of the image to show a five line menu. One option is Document Size that displays two values. The first is the size of the file if it's flattened to remove Layers data. The second is the value including Layers data and Channels.

Dodge tool

Works like the darkroom dodging device. Hold the paddle over your image and the areas it covers will become lighter.

The palette's options includes a menu to set for dodging midtones, highlights or shadows, along with an opacity setting to vary the strength of the dodging effect.

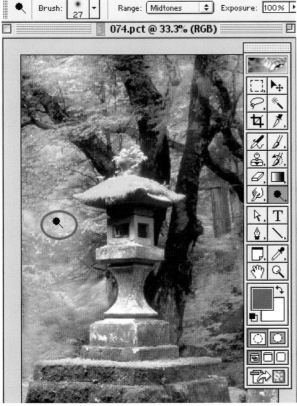

The dodge tool has been used on this image to produce a mist like appearance.

Droplet

MENU   FILE →
        AUTOMATE →
        CREATE DROPLET

This new feature on Version 6 creates a droplet based on pre recorded action. The droplet is an icon that appears on the desktop that you drag a picture on to to automatically process the pre-recorded action. You may want to set it up to adjust a digital camera picture. Here you could pre-record an action that changes the resolution from 72dpi to 240dpi, adds a faint orange hue to give a feeling of warm and a touch of Unsharp mask to improve the digital image.

Dots per inch (DPI)

The measurement used to determine printer and monitor resolution. A 200dpi printout means there are 200 dots in every inch. A monitor resolution with 96dpi is better than a 72dpi one, and so on.

Drop shadow

MENU   LAYER →
        EFFECTS →
        DROP SHADOW

Photoshop 6 makes creating drop shadows a doddle. All you do is make a selection, go to the filter and apply the shadow. From the palette menu you can choose the Blend mode, opacity, angle, distance, blur and intensity – play around until you're happy with the results.

Duotone mode

MENU   IMAGE →
**   MODE →**
**   DUOTONE**

Grayscale images display up to 256 shades of grey, but a printing press only reproduces around 50 levels per ink. Grayscale images printed with black ink look coarser than ones printed with two or more inks.

Duotones are images with two colors that increase the tonal range of a grayscale image and look stunning when subtly applied. When black is used for shadows and grey for midtones and highlights you produce a black & white image. Versions printed using a colored ink for the highlights produce an image with a slight tint that significantly increases its dynamic range.

You need to be in grayscale mode before you can enter the world of Duotones (Image→Mode→Grayscale). Choose a Duotone pre-set by clicking on Load and locate it in the Goodies folder (all the examples here are supplied pre-sets), or create your own color by clicking on the colored ink squares to call up the color wheel.

Select a color you like and watch the bar at the base of the palette appear as a range of hues from black to white. If you stumble across a Duotone color effect you'd like to keep click on save and put the *.ado file in a folder. It can then be called up from the Load option when required. **(See Tritones and Quadtones)**

You can edit the duotone curve by clicking on it to bring up a new dialogue box. Moving the curve right makes colors print heavier in the shadows while moving it to the left makes colors print lighter in highlights.

Duplicating images

MENU   IMAGE →
DUPLICATE Opens up an identical copy of the image and keeps the original open. You can also use the drag & drop method to duplicate one image onto another and avoid using up any RAM. Just click on the image you want to copy, hold down the mouse and drag the cursor over to the destination canvas. If, as in this example, you drag a color image onto a black & white one it will be automatically converted.

Duplicating layers

MENU LAYER →
DUPLICATE LAYER Adding a duplicate layer in the same image is useful when you want to produce complex multi-layered images using Blend modes. Layers can also be duplicated from one image into another using the same drag & drop technique, as described in duplicating images, or copied and pasted.

Tip
● Hold down the Alt key as you duplicate the image to add 'copy' automatically to the end of the title.

Dust & Scratches filter
(See Noise filter)

Edges

An edge is formed where adjacent pixels have high contrasting values. Photoshop has a number of filters that detect these and apply contrast reducing or increasing effects to soften or sharpen the image accordingly.

The top half of the picture (left) is an enlarged part of the stem of the plant in the picture above.

The Find Edges filter picks up all the areas of edge contrast and produces an almost posterized version that highlights these edges.

Emboss filter
(See Stylize filters)

Eraser

Use this to remove pixels, replacing them with the back-ground color, or to a previous state using the Erase to History option, or to an underlying layer.

The Eraser options bar lets you select the opacity of the Eraser and can be set to gradually fade out in a selected number of steps.

You can choose from four brush styles including Paintbrush, Airbrush, Pencil and Block and also vary the size of these from the Brush options box.

The Paintbrush has a Wet Edges option that produces a stronger effect towards the edges of the brush stroke.

Exclusion mode
(See Blending modes)

Exporting from clipboard

As with most programs that handle pictures and text when you copy an item it is saved in the program's clipboard. Photoshop is just the same, so pictures can be copied and then pasted into other programs

Exporting files

MENU   **FILE →**   Photoshop comes
          EXPORT   with two plug-in
modules to export files to GIFs (using File→Save for Web or Paths to Adobe Illustrator. Paths to Illustrator converts Photoshop paths created with the Pen tool into Illustrator files.

Exposure correction

When an image is too dark or too light, caused by either poor scanning or a badly exposed original, it can be corrected using several Photoshop features.
(See Levels, Curves and Brightness)

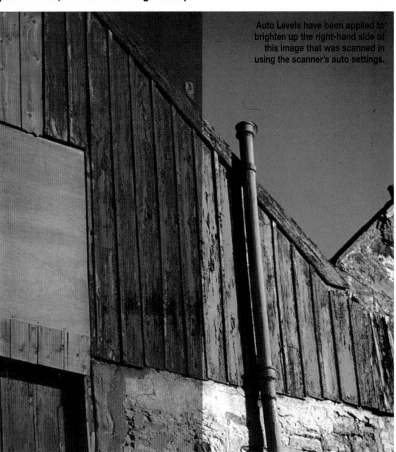

Auto Levels have been applied to brighten up the right-hand side of this image that was scanned in using the scanner's auto settings.

Extract

MENU   **IMAGE** ➜ This feature, **EXTRACT** introduced on Photoshop 5.5, makes selecting objects from their background much easier and is especially useful on complex cutouts such as hair.

You first draw around the edge that you want to cut out using the Edge Highlight tool. Then fill the inner area with the Fill tool. When you click 'preview' the command goes to work and produces a foreground cut out on a transparent background.

If you're happy with the preview cut out click on OK and the extraction is applied. In a few moments you are delivered a cut out that can then be dropped onto another background.

Version 6 has a few new features added to make the selection process even easier. Draw around the edge using the Smart Highlight tool and it calculates how easy it is to select the object and adjusts the thickness of pen to suit. If the edge detail is complex it makes the pen line thicker and if the edge is well defined the pen line becomes thinner.

Paint over the edge that you want to cut round ensuring foreground and background areas are both covered by the highlighter. Use a larger sized highlight brush to paint over areas that aren't easy to define such as the hair where fine strands appear. Select a smaller size brush for the definite edges such as this girl's blouse.

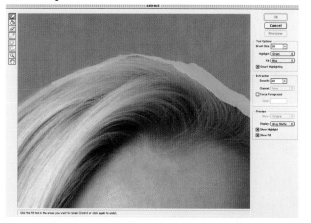

The new Smart Highlight tool automatically adjusts pen thickness as you draw around the subject you want to extract.

Cutting round the hair on this photo could be really difficult to do using one of the normal Selection tools.

When the selection is complete click in the centre, using the bucket/fill tool and then click on preview to see the extraction take place.

Depending on the speed of your computer's processor and the size of the image this could take a few minutes, or longer, to perform the task.

The extracted image can be viewed in a number of ways. The pre-set version appears with a transparent background, but you can also select a grey, white (middle) or black matte (right) which are often more useful to display how good the cutout is. You can also select your own colour, using the colour picker. Version 6 even has an option to view the cut-out as a mask (far left).

It helps to look at the preview in the mask mode when using the new Clean Up and Edge Touch up editing tools. Both are used after the preview has been made to improve the accuracy of the extraction.

Once you have your extracted subject you can either drop the picture onto an existing canvas or create a new one with an interesting background. Here the green canvas effect was achieved in Photoshop using the Clouds filter, followed by Contrast adjustment, Gaussian Blur and a dark vignette. You could also use one of your own photos as a ready-made background as I have done here with the picture of an old leaded window frame.

Tip
● Some areas of the image that you wanted to keep may have been erased. If this happens set the History brush on to the stage prior to the extraction and paint back the missing pixels.

Eye-dropper

This tool, located on the tool palette, is normally used to select the foreground or background color and the only control you have is selecting the sampling area which can be accurate to one pixel, 3x3 or 5x5. Simply position the dropper end over the area you want to sample and click the mouse to take the sample which becomes the foreground color.

Holding down the Alt key when you click selects the background color. The Eye-dropper also appears in several other palettes, including Replace Color, Color Range, Levels, Curves and Hue/Saturation.

Tip
● Hold down the Alt key while using the Airbrush to convert it into an Eye-dropper.

52

Fade command

MENU	EDIT →
	FADE

The fade feature in the filter menu of Version 5.5 has been moved to the edit menu on Version 6 and now allows any filter or color change to be reduced in strength using this fade control. The effect can also be adjusted using the fade with a Blend mode making the filter appear as though it's on a separate layer to give a completely different feel. Definitely one to experiment with.

The Fresco effect from the Artistic filter menu has created a moody oil painting (middle). The Fade command, set to Luminosity Blend mode, gives added sparkle in the greens which is further enhanced by increasing brightness and contrast (bottom).

The Pencil effect from the Artistic filter menu has created a weak pastel result (left). The Fade command, set to Multiply Blend mode, increases contrast to give more vibrant colouring (above).

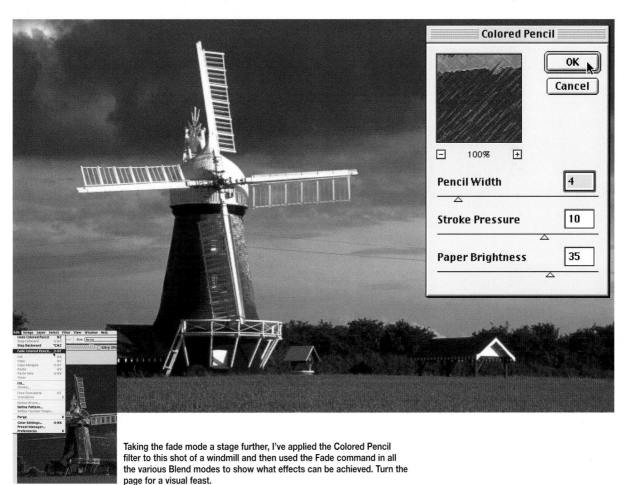

Taking the fade mode a stage further, I've applied the Colored Pencil filter to this shot of a windmill and then used the Fade command in all the various Blend modes to show what effects can be achieved. Turn the page for a visual feast.

f

Feathering

Useful feature that's used to soften the edge of a selection before you cut out or add a filter effect. You control the pixel width of feather from the selection area inwards and outwards. The result is a gradual softening rather than a harsh edge.

A small feather of one or two pixels is all that's need to make a cutout appear less obvious when pasted on a new background. A large feather of around 30 is better when you're adjusting the brightness, contrast or color of a selection within an image. As with most features it's best to try several settings before committing the image to disk.

Feathering can be used to remove red-eye caused by flash or to color the pupils. Above is what happens if you don't feather the selection. Below right has a large feather so the red has bled into the white. A +20 feather gives the best result with, apart from the choice of color, a realistic feel.

File conversion

Photoshop files can be converted into other formats suitable for different uses. When you save an image, select File→Save As and pull down the Save As menu bar in the palette to see a list of file formats to choose from. Then drag the cursor over the one you want to save in that format. Help screens will appear where necessary.

File format

MENU   FILTER →   Digital
          ARTISTIC →   pictures
can be saved in numerous formats, each having distinct advantages, well most do! The JPEG format is one of the most popular, so is TIFF, EPS, GIF and not forgetting Photoshop's very own PSD format. (See the entries of individual file formats.)

f

File info

MENU   FILE →   FILE INFO A dialogue box with several sheets. The first has spaces to add a picture caption, headline and special instructions that can be saved and used on future projects. The second has room to enter key words. Next is the category file, then credits, copyright option and contact details. Each one can be accessed by Caps+1, Caps+2, etc.

File optimizing

You should always optimize pictures when saving them for Web use. The idea is to remove any color that can't be seen be a Web browser as well as resizing to suit the viewing conditions (usually Mac or PC monitor) and saving it all in the most suitable format (usually JPEG or GIF). This is made easier when you use the Save for Web option in Photoshop.

(See Save for Web)

Filling color

Works like the Bucket tool and drops color into the selection. Choose to fill using the foreground or background color in the palette. You can also adjust opacity and select a Blend mode to vary the result.

Tips

● When filling a selection, use the Feather control first to get a softer fill effect (see images below).
● Press the Ctrl+Delete keys to fill the canvas or selection with the foreground color.
● Press Alt+Delete to fill the selection with the background color.

Filters

These are effects that change the look of the photograph by altering the pixels. There are many filters supplied with Photoshop, but many more can be added from third party developers. Filters are found in the – surprise, surprise – filter menu and are listed individually in this book.

The filter effect, and time taken to apply it, will vary on the number of pixels in the picture. A low resolution picture (above left) will process quickly, but the effect may be very harsh, whereas a high resolution image (right) will have a more subtle result.

Tips

● Some filter effects are very memory intensive and can take ages to apply. There's nothing more annoying than waiting for an effect to materialise to be disappointed by the result. To save time make a selection of a key part of the image and apply the filter to this small area.

If the effect works undo it by clicking on the previous state in the history palette or use the Undo (command+Z) shortcut.

Fill Layer

MENU   LAYER →
        NEW FILL LAYER A time
saving
feature that was introduced
on V6.0 which creates a new
layer with either a full color,
gradient or pattern fill. To
show one of its uses I've
selected a sky and will add
a fill layer with a foreground
to transparent gradient.

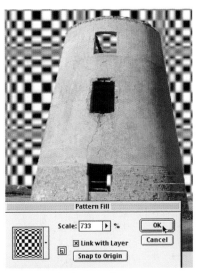

Setting the
foreground color to
black will introduce a
dark and moody
gradient (below),
while orange gives a
sort of sunset effect
(left).You could also
add a pattern fill
(right)...but not for
this shot!

Fit image

MENU   **FILE ➜**
     AUTOMATE ➜
     FIT IMAGE

A new automated feature that resizes the image so that it will fit within a certain pre determined canvas space. If, for example, you have the measurements set to 680x480 and apply fit image command to a 600x600 picture it would reduce it to 480x480. This helps when you need to resize pictures to suit a newsletter or catalogue format with predetermined picture boxes.

Here a landscape format of 640x480 pixel measurements was selected to suit viewing on a basic monitor. This reduced the height of the portrait format picture to 480 pixels.

Flatten image

MENU   **LAYER ➜**
     FLATTEN IMAGE

Images with individual layers can only be saved in the Photoshop PSD file format and need to be merged (flattened) if you want an alternative format. Merging layers reduces the size of the file so it's worth doing if you're totally happy with your results.

In this example eleven layers are used which result in a 25Mb image (above). When merged the file size becomes just 5.72Mb (below).

Tip

● If you want to keep the image with layers but need a version in another file format, choose File➜Save a Copy to create a flattened duplicate.

Foreground color

The foreground color is used to paint, fill and stroke selections and appears as the upper square in the toolbox. You can change the color by either sampling from an image using the Eye-dropper, clicking on the colored square to call up the color picker, or choosing Window➜ Show color to bring up the Color palette.

Freehand Pen tool
(See Pen tools)

Full screen mode

If, like me, you have loads of desktop icons floating around untidily and, often, several applications open at once you may find it becomes difficult to work with Photoshop and its many palettes. The full screen mode, selected from the tool bar, removes all the clutter to make it much easier to see the image. Choose full screen with menu items when you need to access modes or full screen when working on a picture. The F key runs through each option in a cycle.

Fuzziness setting

A similar feature to Tolerance that determines how many colors are selected by the Eye-dropper tool in the Color Range mode. Sliding the control to the right increases the fuzziness and allows a larger range of colors to be picked.

In this example I have taken a sample from the flower's stemen using the Eye-dropper tool and a high fuzziness setting of 161. The preview shows that the selection includes all the tips of the stemen and part of the flower.

The same example with a lower fuzziness setting of 36 has just picked up parts of the stemen head and none of the flower at the base.

Tips

- Avoid high fuzziness levels – they create blurred edges and settings too low can cause jagged edges and miss selected pixels.
- Keep your finger held down on the mouse button as you move around the preview image with the Eye-dropper icon. This will continually adjust the selection.

g

Gamut warning

MENU   VIEW →

GAMUT WARNING

QUICK KEYS **SHIFT+CTRL+Y**

The range of colors a computer monitor can display is known as the gamut and the monitor's gamut has a larger range of colors than a printer can output. If you don't watch out the vivid colors you've been editing will appear from the printer looking dull and lifeless. The Gamut warning's job is to prevent disappointment when you work in RGB mode. It does so by highlighting all the pixels that are out of gamut so you can modify the color before printing. Go to File→ Preferences→ Transparency & Gamut to adjust the way the warning works.

A small exclamation mark also appears above the color in the Color Picker and Color palette when a color is out of the printer's gamut.

Gaussian Blur
(See Blur filter)

GIF format

A GIF (Graphics Interchange Format) is an image with a reduced palette of 256 colors or less that's ideal for viewing on the Web. Photoshop files can be converted to GIFs using File→Save As, File→Export or from within Adobe's Image Ready program which is now supplied as part of Photoshop. GIFs can be saved as normal or interlaced versions that appear gradually on screen as they download from the Web.

Glass filter
(See Distortion filter)

Global light

MENU   **LAYER →**
        LAYER STYLE →
        GLOBAL LIGHT

Several layer effects, such as Drop Shadow and Inner Bevel, give you control over the angle of lighting. Selecting Global lighting ensures that all the layer effects have the same lighting angle so the result looks more natural. If you don't want all the layer effects to be uniform go into the effect you want to have its own light and turn off the use global lighting option.

Glow effect

MENU   **LAYER →**
        EFFECTS →
        OUTER/INNER
        GLOW

A glow effect looks particularly effective when produced around type and can be made to appear from inside or outside the selection in any color. The mode is great for creating fancy head lines for Web sites or newsletters

You can also control the opacity, blur and intensity of the glow along with the Blend mode from within the Effects palette.

Gradient Mask

MENU **LAYER →**
      ADD LAYER MASK

Adding a Gradient Mask to a layer makes the image take on the gradient when blending with other layers. This is useful for complex image creation.

g

Gradient tool

Interesting skies, colorful backgrounds and rainbows are all easily created by selecting the Gradient icon from the toolbox. This brings up a choice of five gradient patterns, from the options bar,

that include Linear, Radial, Angular, Reflected and Diamond – each designed to create a smooth blend from one color to another. Double clicking on the icon brings up the dialogue box where the gradient effect can be edited. As with many Photoshop palettes you can adjust the opacity and the Blend mode to control the effect the gradient has on the base image. There's also a selection of pre-set color gradients to choose from, or you can edit your own.

To create the Gradient Fill just click on the image at the desired start point, drag to the end point and release to flood the image with color.
If you don't like the effect Undo (Ctrl+Z) and start again.

Tips
● To have more control of where the gradient begins reduce the picture so you can draw the gradient line outside the picture area. In this example It's made the gradient less harsh.

Gradient Editor

The Gradient editor is called up when you click on the gradient currently displayed in the brush tool bar. From the editor you can select any of Photoshop's predesigned gradients and edit these or make your own from the start. You can select any color and adjust its position on the scale. The bottom sliders control the position of the color and the top ones the strength, or opacity, of the color.

Gradient Map

MENU **IMAGE →**
ADJUST →
GRADIENT MAP

This converts a color image to grayscale and then lets you apply one of the pre-selected gradients to replace the grey tones with new, posterized colors. You can edit the gradient and watch the preview to help achieve the desired result. The left color replaces blacks the right one replaces whites and any in the middle will replace grey tones. It's like having full control of the posterization mode and a touch of Unsharp mask to improve the digital image.

Grain

Film-like grain can be added to pictures using either the Noise filter or the Diffuse Glow with the Glow slider turned down and Grain increased. You could also try creating your own grain pattern and adding it as a layer using a Blend mode.

Graphic tablet

A graphic tablet such as the Wacom Graphire has a special pen that replaces the computer mouse to control the on-screen cursor. Using a pen gives you much more natural control and makes it much easier to draw or paint and trace around objects when making cut outs.

Photoshop has support for most tablets and using one opens up some extra features such as pressure sensitivity when using the airbrush. These appear on the options bar along the top of the image.

The pen can often be reversed so the other tip can be used as an erasor.

Tablets can go up to sizes as large as A3 which are used by designers. There's even one available that displays the image so you can draw around the actual picture.

Grayscale mode

Produces an image made up of 256 grey tones from black to white. You can't adjust Hue or Saturation in this mode, but Brightness and Contrast can be controlled. Use this mode to convert original color images to black & white.

Tip
● An image converted from color to grayscale may look a little flat. Adjust levels to brighten up the tones.

Grid

MENU	VIEW →
	SHOW/HIDE GRID
QUICK KEY	**Ctrl+'**

A non-printing grid of horizontal and vertical lines that's used to arrange elements symmetrically within an image and to straighten up sections, making it perfect for use with the Transform→Perspective feature.

Selections snap to the grid so it's easier to create and align the same sized boxes.

It can be difficult to edit a picture when the grid is turned on because the lines may get in the way. Using the quick keys to switch back and forth will make it easier to work.

Tip

● Select View→Snap To Grid and the painting tools will follow the grid making it easy to paint in straight lines.

Guides

MENU	VIEW →
	SHOW/HIDE GUIDES
QUICK KEY	**Ctrl+;**

These are horizontal or vertical lines that can be pulled out from the edge rulers to appear over the image. If the rulers aren't visible go to View→Show Rulers.

Guides can be used to align text or for laying out parts of the image in a symmetrical pattern. Go to Preferences→Guides & Grid to choose the guides' color and style (straight or dotted line). The guides will not print and can be removed or repositioned using the Pointer tool.

As with the Grid, Paint tools will snap to the guides if the Snap to Guides option is selected from the View menu.

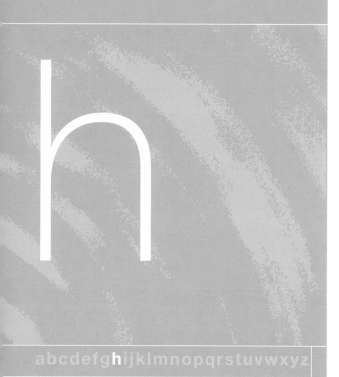

Hard light
(See Blending modes)

Highlights

The brightest parts of the image with detail that will still print. These can be adjusted using the clear triangle on the slider control that appears on the right-hand side of the Levels graph.

Histogram

MENU   IMAGE →   A graph that
        HISTOGRAM   plots the image in a series of pixel values from 0 (black) to 255 (white) and looks like a mountain range profile.

The horizontal scale represents shadow to highlight detail and the vertical axis is the number of pixels at a particular point. You can view the histogram of each of the RGB channels individually or as a group. It's used to check whether your image is suitable for printing and can be edited in the Levels palette by adjusting highlight, shadow and midtone sliders.

A low key image appears with most of the peaks concentrated in the shadow area at the left-hand side.

A high key image has the peaks in the highlight area to the right.

The average tone image should have a graph that rises from the far left, peaks across the middle section and falls to the far right.

Help

Photoshop 6.0's help menu has new brighter interface and, as well as linking to all the stuff provided on the CD that comes with the program, it goes direct to the Web as an extra resource. This ensures we can keep on top of the program and receive any updates that Adobe throw at us.

History brush

Use this to paint in details from a previous stage of editing. Click on the box that appears in the History palette at the stage in the image editing process that you'd like to apply and paint onto the new level.

This is a great option if you're considering hand-coloring a black & white image. Cheat by starting off with a color image and convert it first to grayscale to discard all color information and then back to color. The black & white image can then be colored using the History brush. Click on the left of the opening image to turn on the History brush icon. Then click on the latest stage and begin to paint.

Tip

● Set the brush opacity to around 50%, turn the Impressionist feature on and brush erratically over the image for a surrealistic watercolor wash.

History palette

Every task you perform in Photoshop 5+ is recorded as a step, or state, in the History palette. This allows you to go back up to 100 previous stages when an image you're working on starts to go wrong. A slider on the left-hand side can be dragged slowly through the

stages to help you find when things start to go wrong. Simply click on the last stage that you were happy with and start again to change history – if it was just that simple in life!

Hue

MENU   IMAGE ➔
             ADJUST ➔
             HUE/
             SATURATION

Hue is the image color and varying the Hue slider changes the overall color. The scale runs through the colors of the rainbow starting at the left with blue.

    This picture of wildflowers shows the effect the Hue slider has over the color when adjusted in 30 unit increments.

Hue: 0 (Original)

Hue: +180

Hue: +150

Hue: +60

Hue: +30

Hue: −90

Hue: −120

h

Hue: +120

Hue: +90

Hue: –30

Hue: –60

Hue: –150

Hue: –180

Image Assistant

A new feature to Version 6 that offers, currently, two assistants (wizards) that guide you through a task that you may be struggling to understand. Export transparent image and resize image will no doubt be joined by many more soon.

Image Ready™

Image Ready™ is a Web image editing program that's bundled with Photoshop. It has the same interface and allows seamless connection from within the program.

Photoshop 5.5 came with Version 2, Photoshop 6 comes with Version 3. The program allows you to slice a picture up so that it can be used more effectively on a Web page. You can also optimize pictures, create rollovers and edit animation.

Image resolution

The measure of digital image quality, usually in pixels per inch (ppi). The more pixels per inch the higher the resolution. Lens quality also affects overall image quality.

The resolution only needs to be as good as the viewing media. If, for example, you're only ever going to look at the images on a computer monitor you only need a resolution of 72dpi for Macs and 96dpi for a PC. If, on the other hand, you're wanting to send the images to a magazine or book publisher you'll need a resolution of at least 300dpi. Most desktop inkjet printers require between 150 and 240dpi files.

Image size

MENU   **IMAGE →**
        ADJUST →
        IMAGE SIZE

Is the physical size of the file, measured in kilobytes (K) or megabytes (Mb), that appears at the bottom left of your image. The larger and more complex an image the bigger its file will be. As an example, a simple 4x6in grayscale image, saved at 175dpi, has a file size of around 700K. The same file saved as an RGB increases to just over 2Mb and as a CMYK image to nearly 3Mb. A 300dpi 10x8in image suitable for magazine repro is 27.5Mb. Start adding Layers, or a History palette, and the file could quadruple in size.

You can either resize or resample a picture in Photoshop. Resizing allows you to adjust the number of pixels per inch and keeps the same amount of data by adjusting the dimensions to suit the new pixel setting. Resampling keeps the same dimensions and removes or adds pixels to reach the new pixel setting you key in. Increasing the number of pixels is usually referred to as interpolation.

Shows the size of the image in pixels or percentages. A link appears at the side when Constrain Proportions is on.

Gives size of output file. Can be set to inches, centimetres, pixels or percentages. A link appears when Constrain Proportions is turned on.

When turned on it ensures that the proportions of the width and height are maintained as one of the two values is changed.

When turned off, the file size is maintained. So, as you increase output resolution the file size dimensions are reduced.

If Resample Image is on the file size changes using interpolation. You then have a choice of three methods of resampling.

Tips

● Merge Layers to reduce the image's file size, but only when you're totally happy with the result as it can't be returned to a Layers state at a later date. (See Flatten image)

● Don't work with images larger than you need. Going to Image→Image size and resampling to a smaller size saves space.
● Images only need to be 72dpi for viewing on computer and TV monitors. They should be between 150dpi and 240dpi for printing from most inkjet printers and 300dpi for magazine reproduction.
   Save at the maximum size you intend viewing/printing out.

Indexed colors

Color mode used to reduce the image to 8-bit to suit viewing on older monitors or on the Web to keep the file size conveniently small.

Several color palettes can be selected from the menu including a Web palette with 256 colors that's widely used by Web browsers so your image will look the same whichever computer platform or Internet explorer the picture is viewed on.

Two pictures of trees A and B. A is the original 16.7 million color image. B is index color with just 256 colors. At a glance they look similar. Enlarge just a small portion of the image and you'll see the lack of smooth gradation between colored pixels.

256 colors is fine for Web use, but when making prints stick with maximum color depth.

Info palette

MENU   WINDOW → Basic
        SHOW INFO palette
that displays RGB and CMYK information for the image being worked on. Moving any tool across the image will change the value on screen as it passes over each pixel. The palette also shows X and Y co-ordinates and the width and height of any box or rectangular section that you create.

Input

Inputting pictures into the computer can be done in a number of ways. The fully digital route is to use a digital camera which can be connected to the serial port, or more recently the USB port.

Alternatively the memory card can be taken out of the camera and slotted into a card reader that's like a small drive connected to the parallel or USB port. Some of the latest cameras even have infrared transmission.

If you have a traditional camera and shoot negative film or transparencies you can buy a film scanner that converts the film image into a digital file and connects to the computer's SCSI, USB or parallel port.

A flatbed scanner is like a mini photocopier, designed to scan flat artwork such as prints. They're available to fit in USB, parallel or SCSI ports.

Another option is to have the films scanned by a lab. Many shops now offer Kodak's Picture CD service where the films are processed as normal but you also get a CD with the images. **(See Picture CD)**

Finally you could have a shop scan your photos and place them on a Web server that looks after your images. You can then log on the site and download the pictures you want to print.

Interpolation

If you change the size of a digital file your software either adds pixels when increasing the size or removes them when making the image smaller. This is known as Interpolation and relies on Photoshop knowing which pixels to add or dump.

There are three methods of interpolation – Nearest Neighbour, Bilinear and Bicubic. One can be set as default by going to File→Preferences→General.

Nearest Neighbour offers the fastest method by copying the adjacent pixels, but results are often poor. Bilinear looks at pixels above and below plus left and right and averages out the result to give an intermediate pixel and a smooth blend. It's slower than Nearest Neighbour, but not as slow as Bicubic which looks at all the pixels surrounding each pixel and averages them all out to create the new ones. It then boosts contrast between each pixel to reduce softness.

This photo of an eye is 29 pixels wide by 29 pixels high. Increasing the image to create a 290x290 version requires a hefty interpolation job, and it's a good test for the various methods.
A: Near Neighbour,
B: Bilinear, and
C: Bicubic.

Inverse

| MENU | SELECT → |
| | INVERSE |

When the subject is difficult to draw round accurately, look at the background or surrounding pixels. Could Color Range be used, or the Magic Wand? If so, select the surrounding areas and then the Inverse command to swap to the subject.

Inverting

MENU	IMAGE →
	ADJUST →
	INVERT
QUICK KEYS	CTRL+I

Changes a color negative image into a positive and vice versa.

As a negative you can still apply other filter effects – this example is Find Edges followed by Fade Find Edges at 100% with Difference blend selected.

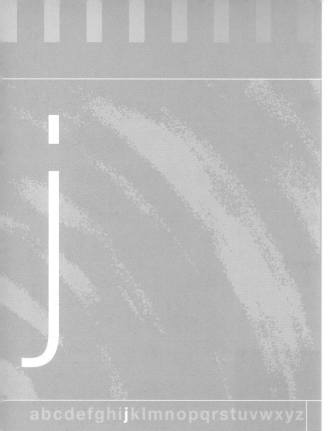

j

abcdefghijklmnopqrstuvwxyz

JPEG
Joiner

JPEG

Short for Joint Photographic Experts Group. The most popular method of image compression that's great for continuous tone photographs.

It supports CMYK, RGB and grayscale. It's a lossy compression method so information is discarded to save disk space, but when saved at a minimal compression level the image can be indistinguishable from the original.

The JPEG Options palette has a slider to adjust the compression level from 0 low quality/high compression to 10 high quality/low compression.

You also have three format options – Baseline Standard for normal use, Baseline Optimized, a higher compression method used for saving images for Web use, and Progressive also for Web use. This option displays the image in stages so the viewer can skip by if the photo isn't interesting.

Warning

● Every time you close and reopen a JPEG file you compress and uncompress, and the affect can be cumulative so the image may gradually decrease in quality. Work in PSD format until you've done everything you want to the image then save to JPEG.

Joiner

A traditional photo technique is to take a series of pictures from the same position but with a different view for each. Then the photographer would mount the images side by side to create a 'joiner', or panorama. This can be done manually in Photoshop using the graduated masks and the clone stamp, but it's easier to do it using auto software such as Stitch or PhotoVista.

1 Select a series of pictures that have been taken for the panorama.

2 Import them into a program such as PhotoStitch.

This sign shows the effect of JPEG compression. The original uncompressed file has a file size of 2Mb. Watch what happens to the file size and the quality as higher compression is chosen.

JPEG, maximum quality, setting 10, file size 1.1Mb. It's hard to spot any difference with this and the uncompressed file.

JPEG, high quality, setting 7, file size 392K. Very subtle changes in color of some pixels, but still very good.

Cropped version of original.

JPEG, medium quality, setting 4, file size 228K. It's now starting to clump groups of pixels in blocks noticeable in the outlined area.

JPEG, low quality, setting 0, file size 104K. Low quality produces poor results and the recognizable problems of heavy compression.

You can use Photoshop to stitch pictures manually. Extend the canvas to the same length of the total length of the pictures you are joining. Paste them onto the canvas and position them. Reduce the opacity of the top one so you can see where it overlaps and adjust so they match. Use the gradient tool to get a good blend. Then use the Clone tool to help patch up bad bits. Repeat this on all the pictures. It's far easier to use an auto stitching program though.

3 Left & above: let the software automatically stitch the photos together. You may then have to crop and clone in the blank spots.

4 The result is an impressive panorama.

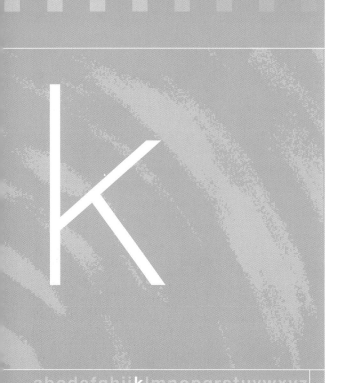

k

Keyboard shortcuts

Shortcuts to commands and options using individual or groups of keys. Learn the ones you use regularly to speed up your work. When shortcuts are available they're listed in this book as Quick Keys.

Knockout

A mode from the Blend options palette selected from the Layer Style menu that allows you to be more creative with the ways layers react with other layers. It can be used with text to great effect. In this example I've taken a scan of a hand, added a red blue layer and then the top layer is the text I will 'Knockout'

Knockout selected along with all three channels produces a clear base picture through the text. I've added a bevel to the text to lift it from the blue background.

This was essential for the more graphic version below where blend mode was used and a channel removed.

Kodak Photo CD

Kodak were way ahead of their time launching Photo CD in 1992 as a product designed to view photos on a television. Unfortunately it didn't take off until around four years later.

The service is offered by photo finishers and pro bureaux. Your images are scanned at high resolution using drum scan quality and recorded onto disk as Pict files. When you open the disk you have a choice of five file sizes from 192x128ppi to 3072x2048ppi. The smaller sizes are for using as positionals or for TV and Web use and the larger files are for making prints allowing up to around 7x10in enlargements.

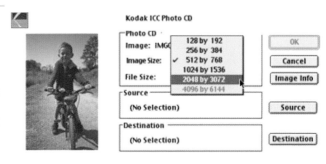

Kodak Picture CD

Similar principle to Photo CD, but with a magazine style interface and free software, produced in association with Adobe and Intel. The CD opens up with a contents page and a range of options. Various menus let you edit and enhance your pictures, send them as e-mail postcards, catalogue them and print them. The service is available when you have a film processed and just requires a tick on the film processing envelope to ensure the lab produces a Picture CD of your film as well as a set of photos.

The interface is extremely friendly and easy to navigate. The first page that appears on screen is the cover of the magazine (above). Clicking the arrow at the bottom takes you to a contents page (left). This lists various options on the CD and your pictures appear on the right with brief captions. Selected pictures can be enhanced using free software (below left) and the print option lets you select single or multiple images to print at various sizes (below right).

Lab Color

An international standard for color measurements developed by the Commission Internationale de L'Eclairage (CIE). It's capable of reproducing all the colors of RGB and CMYK and uses three channels – one for luminosity and the other two for RGB type color ranges.

Some users prefer to work in this mode as it's device independent and colors that fall into the LAB color gamut aren't changed when you convert to CMYK.

Lasso

There are three Lassos to pick from the toolbox.

The two standard versions, Freehand and Polygon, have been joined by a Magnetic version.

The Polygon Lasso is good for drawing round boxes and straight edged items as it creates a straight edge between the source and destination point.

The Freehand Lasso is used in most programs and is used by accurately drawing round the subject. You can select a feather to be applied to the section and turn anti-aliasing on or off.

Magnetic Lasso is arguably the most useful Lasso. You draw roughly around the subject and the Lasso detects contrast changes and defines the edge. It then pulls the inaccurate drawing in to line, often creating a very good selection.

Tip
● Don't worry too much about being spot on with your drawing. You can hold down the Shift key to add to the selection or the Alt key to take away from it.

Layers

MENU **LAYER →**
NEW LAYER →
QUICK KEY **SHIFT+CTRL+N**

One of the most useful features of Photoshop is Layers. Basically, using layers is like having several sheets of tracing paper, each holding part of the image. Laying the sheets on top of each other builds up the image and it's easy to remove any sheet to change the feel of the work. But, being digital, layers offer much more.

You can change how one layer reacts with another using the Blend modes (see individual entries). You can adjust the opacity so one layer is stronger than another, you can apply a filter effect to one layer and you can copy and paste from one layer to another.

Photoshop 6 has a few new Layer options on the palette. A selection of locks can be assigned to a layer to protect it from accidents later. The first is lock transparency. This used to be called Preserve Transparency and ensures that any areas that are transparent (indicated by the chequered grid) will not be affected by paint or filter effects. Then we have lock

paintbrush which, as the name implies, prevents you from using brushes. The third is a lock to stop you using the Move tool to move elements from this layer. All three can be individually selected or locked as a group.

This leaf image has four layers, combined using Blend modes.

Layers are like sheets of glass or tracing paper each one placed on top of the other to produce a combined multi-layer image.

Layer Based Slice

MENU **LAYER →**
NEW LAYER BASED SLICE

Another new feature to Version 6.0 that lets you cut up, or slice, your picture into several pieces. When the image is used in a Web page each slice is saved as an independent file with html code and becomes a fully functional part. The html code contains color palette info and links, rollover effects, and animations can be added in Image Ready. Slices help you gain faster download speeds and increased image quality. Apply a layer based slice on a layer with a selection and the slice will be positioned around it. This can then be moved and scaled using the Move tool.

Layer Clipping Path

MENU   **LAYER →**
ADD LAYER CLIPPING PATH   The Layer clipping
path is a sharp edged shape around an object that can be edited using the Shape or Pen tools. The path can be converted into a layer mask by choosing Layer→Rasterise→Layer Clipping Path

This Layer clipping path was a tick before I started to drag the points around.

Layer Mask

MENU   **LAYER →**
ADD LAYER MASK   A layer mask controls how much of that particular layer appears in the overall image. Black masked areas don't show through and white areas do. You can use the vignette and graduate filters to good effect using Layer Masks.

Masks can be turned off at any stage and any bits of the image that have been masked will show through on the overall image again.

Left: The pagoda has been very roughly cut from its background and pasted on the sky layer. It obviously looks like it has too! By adding a Layer Mask you can paint out areas of the pagoda layer using the Eraser. Use a large eraser brush to get rid of the surrounds and a small one to paint around the edges. If you make a mistake you can paint back using the Airbrush
Below: Okay, this one's not the most stunning creation, but you get the idea!

Layer properties

MENU   **LAYER →**
LAYER PROPERTIES   Opens up a small box where you name the layer and select a color for it.

Layer set

A great new feature of Version 6 that allows layers to be grouped and all the layer blend modes applied to the group. Alternatively the individual layers within the group can have their own set of blend modes that become active when you select Pass Through from the set's blend mode options.

Layer Style

MENU   **LAYER →**
LAYER STYLE   Control how a layer looks by adjusting its style from a new palette. This offers advanced blending options that let you adjust the way each color channel blends with the layer below and each element can be adjusted from the palette. Global light lets all the layers have the same angle and altitude.

Lens Flare

MENU	FILTER →
	RENDER →
	LENS FLARE

Another one of those filters that will make lens manufacturers cringe. They spend millions on research to get a lens that you can point into the light without getting flare and then you go and stick some in using Photoshop! The truth is a touch of flare can sometimes add the extra bit that's needed to make the image work.

Tip

● Try using the fade option after you've applied Lens flare.

The palette offers a choice of three lens types and an adjustable brightness control. There's a preview window to check the result before you apply the effect to the main image.

105mm prime

50-300mm zoom

35mm prime

Levels

MENU	IMAGE →
	ADJUST →
	LEVELS
QUICK KEY	Ctrl+L

Used to adjust the black and white points of an image to change the contrast. When you're in this palette there's a window with the histogram and sliders to control the darkest and lightest points. The left-hand triangle controls the shadow area, the right triangle looks

after the highlights and the middle triangle adjusts midtones.

The original scan is far too dark. This can be resolved in Levels by adjusting the highlight and shadow area markers to improve the dull scan.

Levels
(cont.)

The white point is way beyond the histogram.

Adjust the mid-point.

Go into Levels and adjust brightest to lighten the image.

You can make posterized effects too.

Line art

An image that's drawn using one color on a background color with no midtones. Line art is a popular giveaway on royalty-free CDs, such as this example, taken from IMSI's Masterclips collection – should that be Lion Art!

Lighten mode
(See Blend modes)

Lighting Effects
(see over page)

Line tool

Used to place lines in the image. When you draw with the Line tool it us the foreground color and whatever width is set in the palette. You can change the color, width and style of line from the Options palette. You c also stick on an arrowhead making the tool useful for creating pointers.

Liquify

MENU   IMAGE ➜   LIQUIFY

Some one at Adobe must have been playing around with Kai's Super Goo one weekend and decided Photoshop 6.0 owners would want it. The truth is we probably don't but we will have plenty of fun deciding we don't! It basically lets you smudge pixels to distort the image as if it was liquid and the most fun can be had by creating wacky portraits of people, or pets. Here I've used the Pucker tool to shrink the nose, the Bloat tool to make the eyes and teeth bulge, the Twirl tool to add an artificial curl to the hair and the Warp tool to pull up the edges of the mouth. Not bad eh?…you'll soon get fed up with it! Don't discard it so quickly, though, it does have practical uses. You could use the Bloat tool set to a low pressure and enlarge the eyes just a little to make them look wide open. Or maybe use the warp to turn the corners of the mouth to introduce more of a smile.

Tips

● Use the mesh grid to help show you the extent of effect you've added and change its colour so it stands out from the picture you're working on.

The bloat tool was set to a low pressure and used to enlarge the eye slightly, making it appear a touch wider.

Oh dear, this tool also gives you a licence to create all sorts of what's the point pictures.

Luminosity blend
(See Blend modes)

LZW compression

A lossless method of compression used with with TIFF and GIF file formats to save space without affecting image quality. The disadvantage is it takes longer to open a compressed image than an uncompressed version.

As a matter of fact

● LZW is named after its three inventors Abraham Lempel, Jacob Ziv and Terry Welch. Sounds too odd to be true!

Lighting Effects

MENU **FILTER →**

RENDER →

LIGHTING EFFECTS

A superb range of filters that can be used to simulate various forms of light from spotlight to tungsten. There's plenty to go at so it's a case of picking a suitable image and sliding the controls to experiment. Remember to select undo (Ctrl+U) if you don't like the effect or click on a previous stage in the History palette.

The original was lit by a single studio flash head and softbox from the right. This has given it a fairly decent lighting effect but we can do all sorts of other things. Now where's the light!

The idea behind this version was to create a tungsten spotlight effect. The light type was set to spotlight with an intense but narrow, white beam and the ambient light was yellow with a positive ambience setting to create the warmth.

Omni light was selected with white light at a medium intensity. The point was positioned on the white flower to create a glowing effect. The ambient light was set to blue to contrast and give a wintery feel to the shot.

A spotlight effect with dark tones can be used to place emphasis on one area of the photograph. In this case drawing attention to the group of fish to the right.

Directional lighting was used here with a red light set to full intensity. The ambient light was set to underexpose and green which has merged the colours to give a subtle orange feel.

Here Omni lighting was positioned to the right and both colour boxes were set to purple they combine to give a very dark feel with the single flower highlighted with a brighter tone.

A pre-set effect that gives a stage-like effect and shows the extent of the range of styles available from the Lighting filters. You can alter each light point individually for angle and width of light source.

Omni lighting was used with grey and black colors so the background pixel colors have an effect on the lighting. The idea was to create a moonlight effect, and a quick tweak in color balance will sort it.

m

Magic Eraser

Introduced on Photoshop 5.5, this tool, found in the Eraser compartment of the toolbox, is used to make pixels transparent. Click on the area you want to lose and the pixels disappear.

The palette has a number of options including the Opacity and Tolerance levels along with on/off options for anti-aliasing, Use all Layers and Contiguous modes.

Anti-aliasing makes some of the edge pixels semi-transparent to ensure edges of unremoved details are smooth for natural cutouts. Using All Layers mode makes pixels in every layer be considered by the Eraser. Contiguous mode ensures just the pixels connected to the sampled color are selected. When turned off, any pixels with a similar value within the image are selected.

All this image needed was six clicks in various parts of the sky to completely remove it. When pasted onto another background it will show through in all the areas of transparency.

Turning Anti-aliasing on (right) ensures that edge pixels appear softer which, in turn, makes the cutout look more natural.

Magic Wand

Click on the image using
this tool to select an
area that has the same
brightness. If for
instance your subject
has a blue background
that you want to change
to green, click anywhere
on the blue and you'll
see the Magic Wand
creates a selection
around all the pixels that
have a similar color and
brightness level. Adjust
the Tolerance setting to
increase or decrease the range in the selection. You can also
select from an individual channel which is sometimes easier.

Tip

● Holding down the Shift key as you click using
the Magic Wand adds to the selection and holding
down the Alt key removes from the selection.

Magnetic Pen
(See Pen tools)

Magnification box

Appears at the bottom
left of a picture and lets
you enter a value
manually to change the
size of the
image on
screen.

Enlarging the
image on screen
helps when you
need to edit
small areas of
detail, but this
may appear as
blocks of pixels
so you should
use the Zoom
tool to nip
backwards and
forwards.
**(See Zoom
tool)**

Above: Image
viewed on screen
at 100%. Right:
Image viewed at
maximum 1600%.

Marquee Tool

The marquee tool is used to make a
rectangular or circular selection around
the subject. Then copy and paste can
be used to pick up and drop the
selection elsewhere.

Tip

● Use the Marquee tool to create lovely vignette
effects by adding a large feather to the selection
before you copy and paste to a blank document.

Masks

Used to protect
parts of the image
when you apply filter
effects or change
color. They can be
added to channels
or layers. Select the
mask from the
Channels palette
and the foreground
and background
colors appear in
grayscale. You can
then use the Paint
and Eraser tools to
add to or remove
parts of the mask.

You can also save
your own selections
as masks by going to Select→Save Selection. This creates an
Alpha channel that you can rename and use later. A mask
created in the Alpha channel makes it easy to bring back
complex selections. Go to Select→Load Selection to produce
a selection where the black parts of the mask meet the white
parts. This can be applied to any layer or channel.

m

Measure

The measure tool is an under used item that is used to give precise details about subject distance and angle. It can also be the perfect assistant when you need to straighten up a wonky horizon or leaning wall. Click on it and draw a line along the sloping object. Then go to Image→Rotate Canvas Arbitrary and the image will magically straighten up.

Median filter
(See Noise filter)

Memory

Photoshop is one of the more hungry programs, especially when you have a large History palette and several unmerged layers. As a result if your computer doesn't have loads of RAM spare you could see the performance drop and you may find filters take much longer to apply.

Click on the arrow at the bottom of the window by the file size figures and select Scratch Sizes from the drop down menu. You'll see the figures change. The new left-hand figure represents the room required for the currently opened images and the right-hand one is the space available in RAM. If the first figure is bigger than the second you're treading on thin ground and could find your computer crashes more often.

The computer will borrow memory from the hard drive and will slow down as it accesses the info. Either work with just one image open at a time or upgrade your PC and buy some more RAM. **(See RAM)**

Merging Layers

When you've finished editing an image and are sure you don't need to keep it in layers you can flatten the layers to make the image's file size much smaller. There are several ways to do this – all found near the bottom of the Layers menu.

Merge Layers and Merge Down combine the selected layer and the one below it in the Layers palette. Merge Visible combines all layers with an eye icon in front of the layer's name in the Layers palette.

Merge Linked brings together all the layers that you've selected using the linking box. Merge Group combines all the layers that you've previously grouped using the Layer→Group Linked command. Flatten Image merges all layers that are visible and discards all the others. It's the option to choose when all your image editing is complete.

Mezzotint filter
(See Pixelating filters)

Moiré patterns

A mottled pattern caused when printed material is converted to digital using a scanner. Some scanning software has a descreening feature that eliminates the pattern but this can soften the image.

You can also rotate the material to be scanned slightly in the scanner and straighten it up once scanned, which sometimes helps.
(See Noise filters)

Moiré patterns
(cont.).

This scan of a Peacock butterfly came from a 2x1in picture in a magazine. The Moiré pattern isn't obvious when the picture is small, but as soon as you enlarge it the criss-cross pattern is harsh. Use Photoshop's Median filter at a setting of around two to reduce the pattern.

Montage
A collection of images and text brought together on one canvas using features such as Layers, Blending modes and the Rubber Stamp tool to make seamless joins.

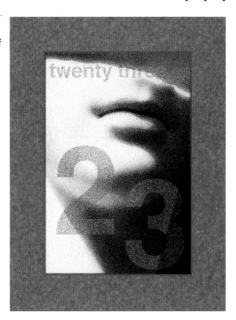

Motion Blur
(See Blur modes)

Move tool
Hardly the most exciting item in the Photoshop toolbox, yet still useful. It's used to drag the image around on screen and can also be used to move Selections and Layers across to other Photoshop images.

Double click on the tool to call up the Options palette and just two options Pixel doubling and Auto Select Layer. Turn Pixel doubling on to increase the speed the tool moves the selected image in the preview. Auto Select Layer makes the tool automatically select your image's top layer.

Just to prove two heads are better than one! The better expression was borrowed and blended into the other image.

Multi-page PDF to PSD

MENU   FILE →
        AUTOMATE →
        MULTI-PAGE
        PDF TO PSD

A feature introduced with Version 5.5 that automatically converts Acrobat PDF files into Photoshop PSD. White backgrounds become transparent and images can be edited in Photoshop. Options are available to save at various resolutions in color or black & white, as seen here on Photoshop Tutorial PDF files.

Multiply mode
(See Blending modes)

n-o

abcdefghijklm**no**pqrstuvwxyz

Navigator palette
Noise filter
Note

Opacity
Open
Open recent
Options palette
Output levels

Navigator palette

MENU **WINDOW→**
SHOW NAVIGATOR

This palette shows a small preview of the image you're working on. The palette preview can be made smaller or larger by dragging the bottom right edge of the box. At the base of the preview window is a zoom scale that you adjust to make the main image magnify or reduce in size. The area that shows on screen appears as a frame in the navigator's preview window which gets smaller as you increase magnification. The frame can be moved around the preview to select the area of the main image you want to work on.

Noise filter

MENU **FILTER →**
NOISE...

Four filters used to add grain or remove dust in an image to make it look natural.

93

ADD NOISE

When used in small amounts this filter can make a digital picture with smoothed edges or an Illustrator file look more natural. Use in larger amounts to recreate an effect you'd obtain using fast film. Controls include an amount slider to vary from a very subtle 1 to an unbelievably gritty 999. Then you can choose between Uniform or Gaussian distribution. Gaussian produces a stronger effect. Finally turn Monochromatic on or off. When on, the Noise filter works the same on all color channels unlike off where the effect is random on each channel.

Adding 8 units of Gaussian distribution with Monochromatic selected.

Adding 39 units of Gaussian distribution with Monochromatic selected.

Adding 62 units of Uniform distribution without Monochromatic selected.

DESPECKLE

A subtle softening filter that helps reduce noise caused by poor scanning. When applied increase sharpness using the Unsharp Mask filter.

This close-up of a girl's eye was cropped from a 46Mb scan. The Despeckle filter softens the image but does help reduce some of the problems of the scan.

MEDIAN

Used to reduce noise, so it's quite effective with the Moiré patterns that are caused when scanning printed material. The downside is it tends to soften the image. Apply the Unsharp Mask filter to increase sharpness after this filter has been used.

Median has a dialogue box with a sliding adjuster giving more control over the effect. The Moiré pattern is easily removed but the result is softer and needs the Unsharp Mask applying.

Noise filter (cont.)

The most useful of the Noise filter range is Dust & Scratches, especially when used on scanned films. No matter how well you try to keep the surface clean it will attract dust and result in scans with marks.

DUST & SCRATCHES

A noise filter that detects dramatic changes in adjacent pixels and blurs the surrounding colors to smooth out the tones.

It's not always clever enough to know what is and what isn't dust so don't think this is the answer to your prayers. You're more likely to end up with a soft result than a rescued one!

Try various combinations of the two Radius and Threshold sliders and adjust the settings until the best result shows in the preview window. Dragging the Radius slider to the right increases the effect, unlike the Threshold slider that reduces it.

Tips

● Draw a selection around the affected area, apply a feather and then use the Dust & Scratches filter.
● Adjust the zoom ratio of the preview until the area containing the dust or scratch is visible.
● Use the Rubber Stamp tool to clone out larger blots.

Note

A new feature on Version 6 that allows you to leave messages around the picture. These appear as little notes on the image which, when clicked open reveal the message you've left. Useful if you're working with a designer and need him to do something with the picture before it goes to print.

Opacity

The opacity slider appears in many of the palettes and is adjusted by either dragging the arrow left or right or typing in a new percentage value. Use this mode to adjust the layer's appearance in the overall image or adjust strengths of paints and editing tools.

A simple image flipped and enlarged to make it look as though the person is looking over himself. The version above with 100% opacity is too harsh whereas the one below with 45% opacity produces a more effective result.

Opacity set to 20%.

Opacity set to 40%.

Opacity set to 60%.

Opacity set to 80%.

Opacity set to 100%.

Setting text at various opacities can produce interesting results.

Open

MENU   FILE ➔

OPEN

Use this to open pictures from within Photoshop. It will point you to a folder or directory and you then go through the system to search for the picture. When you find the image double click it to open.

Open recent

MENU   FILE ➔   A new feature on version 6 that shows a

OPEN RECENT   list of recently opened images so you don't have to trawl through your entire system if you want to re-open an image you have previously worked.

Options palette

MENU   WINDOW ➔   Double clicking on anything in the toolbox

SHOW OPTIONS   brings up the Options palette that usually has a range of settings, check boxes and sometimes grayed out items that can only be accessed when you're in certain modes. Ones at the bottom with a stylus next to them need a graphics tablet attached to be functional. The arrow at the top right lets you reset the tools.

Output levels

A slider at the base of the Levels palette is used to control the highlight and shadow detail of the image for printing. Dragging the left-hand marker right decreases shadows while dragging the right-hand marker left decreases highlights.

Tip

● If you get a bronzing effect on the blacks of your inkjet prints it's because too much black ink is being used. It occurs on some types of paper when they're not fully compatible with printers. Adjusting the shadow triangle from 0 to 5 or 10 reduces shadow density and helps avoid overinking the black.

Overlay mode
(See Blending modes)

96

p

abcdefghijklmno**p**qrstuvwxyz

Page Setup

MENU   **FILE ➜**
              PAGE SET UP

This takes you to your printer's settings where you select the paper size and orientation. You can also go into advanced Photoshop settings including a Transform option. This allows you to adjust the way Photoshop outputs the result overriding the printer's default settings. By selecting values from black to white you can ensure the image you see on screen is exactly what's printed out. But you have to be prepared to spend a lot of time testing this to get the desired results.

Paint bucket

Use this to flood the selected area with the foreground color.
  The Tolerance setting determines how many pixels are affected by the flood. A small amount results in a patchy paint effect, while a higher tolerance may color areas you don't want covered. The deckchair stripes, above, show the Tolerance at four settings. The left-hand one was set to 10, second 20, third 30 and fourth 40.

Click on Anti-aliased to soften the edge of the paint fill. The stripes, left, show anti-aliased turned on (left stripe) and off (right stripe).

Use all Layers uses pixels in all the layers to influence which ones are filled, but only fills the area on the active layer.

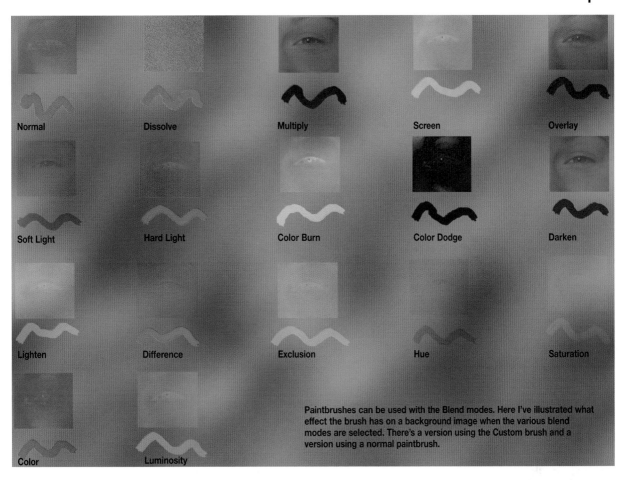

Normal	Dissolve	Multiply	Screen	Overlay
Soft Light	Hard Light	Color Burn	Color Dodge	Darken
Lighten	Difference	Exclusion	Hue	Saturation
Color	Luminosity			

Paintbrushes can be used with the Blend modes. Here I've illustrated what effect the brush has on a background image when the various blend modes are selected. There's a version using the Custom brush and a version using a normal paintbrush.

Paintbrush tool

One of three tools used to apply selected color to the image. The paintbrush can be used on full strength or less using the opacity setting to reduce the amount of color affecting the image. With lower opacity the original pixel color can still be seen. This effect is like adding a wash to the image and is really useful for hand-coloring black & white images.

A paintbrush loaded with various colors was used to roughly handcolor this flower stall. The layer was duplicated and Gaussian blur and Diffuse glow filters where applied to give the glowing effect.

Palettes

The menu boxes that let you adjust settings of various tools.

Arrange them carefully on the desktop to avoid clutter. Many of them have shortcut keys to open and close the window, making it visible or invisible on the desktop.

Palettes can be grouped too to make the desktop even tidier

(See Appendix C)

The palettes have a wide range of options to adjust the way the features work. Spending time getting used to what they have to offer is beneficial.

You can drag one palette onto another to combine them and save space on the desktop.

Paste into

QUICK KEYS SHIFT+CTRL+V Used to paste an image into part of another that's been previously selected. The new pasted image appears within the selection. The area around the selection becomes a Layer Mask and the icon appears by the pasted image by the layer thumbnail.

In this example the sky was pasted into the window area.

Path component selection tool

This tool is used to select a whole path shape and move it on screen. Unlike the direct selection tool which lets you click on an anchor point and drag to distort the path's shape.

Paths

Paths are outlines created by drawing with one of the Pen tools. They are vector based so don't contain pixels and appear separate from a normal bitmap image.

A thumbnail of the path can be viewed in the Paths palette, and from here you can select a number of options to apply to the active layer from a row of icons along the base or from the arrow's drop down menu. These options include: Filling the path with the foreground color; producing a Stroke to add the foreground color along the selected Path and making a Selection from the Path.

A Path can be moved to a new image by dragging the original path icon from the palette and pulling it over a new image. You can also copy paths from one location and paste them into another using the normal copy & paste option. Paths can be converted quickly into selections and selections can be turned into paths.

Paths are also used by designers who turn the selection into a clipping path and import it into a page layout. The clipping path ensures everything outside the frame appears as transparent on the layout. This ensures text wraps around the subject and the subject blends well with the layout.
(See Pen tools)

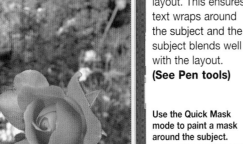

Use the Quick Mask mode to paint a mask around the subject.
Magnify an area and use the Eraser and Airbrush to remove or add to the mask, then convert the masked selection into a path.

One option is to fill the path with the foreground color.

Producing a Stroke to add the foreground color along the selected Path.

Making a Selection from the Path.

Pattern Stamp tool

Like the Clone Stamp, but it takes the sample from a preselected area that you've defined. To use this select an area you want to clone using the Rectangular Marquee and use this to create the pattern. Then select Edit→Define pattern.

Now when you use the Pattern Stamp

tool the defined area will be repeated as you draw across the canvas. If the Align box is checked the pattern will be repeated in uniform tiles in the shape of the selection. If you uncheck the Align box a tile appears

wherever you draw. Blend tools are also available in this mode.

Normal blend

Dissolve blend

Hard Light blend

Difference blend

Luminosity blend

Tip

● Make your own mini gift wrapping paper by selecting a part of a subject that would look good repeated and use the Pattern Stamp tool in aligned mode to cover an A4 or A3 sheet.

Pen tool

With an icon like the nib of an ink pen this tool is used to create a path that can be turned into a selection. It's unusual to use at first, but spend some time getting familiar with it and your drawing and selection skills will improve tenfold.

The Pen tool icon on the toolbar has several options. The first is Pen tool which you use to add points, known as anchor points, around the subject.

The points are automatically linked to make the

path. This is ideal when you want to draw straight lines and smooth curves. You can have as many anchor points as you like and they can be

removed by clicking on them.

To draw a straight line, click at a start point then move to the finish point and click again. To complete a straight path click the Pen tool icon in the toolbox when you reach the end. To complete a round path click on the original starting point to complete the shape.

The Freeform Pen tool is like the normal Lasso and creates a path wherever you draw. It's like using a normal pen and is very accurate, providing you are! Anchor points are added along the path, and their positions can be changed when the path is complete. The Magnetic Pen tool works like the Magnetic Lasso and automatically locates high contrast differences between pixels and lays the path along the edge. This used to be selected from the Tool bar but can now be found on the options bar at the top of the screen. Use this if you're a little unsteady at drawing.

Tips

● When using the Magnetic Pen tool go slowly so the Pen locates the edge you're drawing along to ensure it picks up what you expect it to.
● Hold down the Shift key to create a straight line running at a 45° angle.
● Click the Rubber Band box in the Options palette to see the curve of the path you're about to create as you move the Pen tool.

PDF

Short for Portable Document Format, this file format is used to convert Quark documents that contain words and pictures into a format that any one can view using the free Adobe Acrobat reader. Pictures that have been edited in Photoshop can also be saved in this format.

Pencil tool

Produces a hard-edged line and is more useful for drawing than retouching images. The options palette has a fade feature that gradually reduces the pencil color opacity to zero giving a gradual fading effect. There's also an Auto erase that replaces the image with the background colour as you draw.

Perspective

MENU	EDIT →
	TRANSFORM
	PERSPECTIVE

Use this to either reduce converging verticals or exaggerate them. Drag the handles at the edges of the selection to pull in or pull out the canvas. A tall building that's been taken from a low angle with a wide-angle lens will appear narrower at the top. Stretch the canvas outward to make the walls upright.

Alternatively a road going off into the distance can be made to reach a pinpoint at the horizon by pulling the canvas in at the top.

p

PICT file

Is widely used by Mac operators for use in graphics and page layout programs, and is ideal for transferring between the two. It supports RGB and allows a single Alpha channel, Index colors and Grayscale.

Pixel dimensions

The number of pixels measured along the width and height of an image, quoted, for example, as 640x480ppi on basic digital cameras and 1280x960ppi on megapixel models.

Pixelating filters

MENU   FILTER ➔ A range of
PIXELATE seemingly pointless filters that convert the selected area into varying patterns of clumped pixels.

Picture Package

MENU FILE ➔
AUTOMATE ➔
PICTURE PACKAGE

An auto mode that resizes a selected picture to a specified resolution and fits a variety of sizes on an A4 page, ranging from one to sixteen pictures.

CHOOSE YOUR TEMPLATE
Picture Package has a range of layouts you can choose from. This is a great automated tool to help you print multiple photos from one image on a sheet of A4 paper. It's a shame it won't automatically locate several images and print them together on one sheet – maybe on the next version!

COLOR HALFTONE
Divides the image into rectangles and replaces them with circles to create an enlarged halftone effect. The menu lets you select the radius of the halftone dot, with pixel values from 4 to 127, and you can enter screen-angle values for each channel. It can take ages to apply and you'll wonder why you bothered!

FRAGMENT
Duplicates pixels and offsets them to create an effect that you'd normally only see after a few too many drinks!

CRYSTALLIZE
Takes pixels into lumps and converts them into a polygon shape of solid color. The size of polygon can be varied between 3 and 300 pixels, although anything past 3 starts to look ridiculous.

POINTILLIZE
Makes the image look like a pointillist painting. Yuk!

MEZZOTINT
Brings up a dialogue box that has nine options – each scrambling the picture to look as though it's a badly tuned television picture. One to avoid, unless, of course, you like looking at badly tuned images!

MOSAIC
Clumps pixels into square blocks and makes them the same color. The effect is like a very low resolution image and another one we'll avoid.

FACET
One of the better pixelating filters, changes clumps of similar colored pixels into blocks of the same color pixels to make images look like they're paintings.

Plastic Wrap filter
(See Artistic filters)

Plug-in filters

A filter that offers additional features to the standard program. Photoshop supports third-party filters that can be added to the plug-ins folder to increase the program's flexibility. Many of the current supplied range used to be third-party options.
(See Appendix E)

Many more plug-ins are available as free downloads from Web sites, one of the best being PC Resources for Photoshop at *<www.netins.net/showcase /wolf359/plugins.htm>* **(See Appendix D)**

Posterization

MENU   IMAGE →
         ADJUST →
         POSTERIZE

Converts the image into a number of brightness levels between 2 and 255 to produce a graphic effect. 2 is too harsh, 255 too subtle. A good balance is between four and eight.

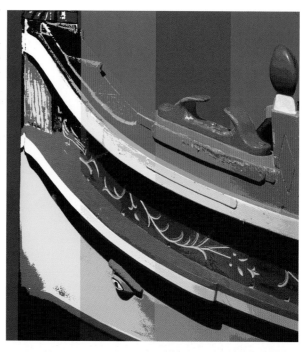

This shows the result of varying levels of Posterization running from the left; 2 levels, 4 levels, 8 levels and 16 levels

Posterization set to 2 levels.

Posterization set to 4 levels.

Posterization set to 6 levels.

Posterization set to 8 levels.

Posterization set to 10 levels.

Preset manager

MENU EDIT → PRESET MANAGER Brings all the preset palettes into one box so you can create new ones, load and edit existing ones or delete unwanted ones.

Preserve luminosity
(See Color balance)

Preserve Transparency
When this box is ticked in the Layers palette the areas of transparency are protected from brush strokes or other changes made to that layer.

Just to show the effect I cut around the duck and pasted it on to a new layer. Then I painted over the duck using Preserve Transparency on the bottom version

Print Options

MENU   **FILE** ➜   At last
       PRINT OPTIONS   Adobe
have come up with a sensible
printing system. Now when you
select this mode you can
choose Scale to fit Media which
automatically adjust the image
to suit the paper you're using in
your printer. A message used to
come up saying Image too big,
do you wish to proceed.

You can also adjust the size and
position of the image so it prints in a certain part of the paper. Show bounding box
lets you adjust by dragging the corner boxes or you could manually adjust size and

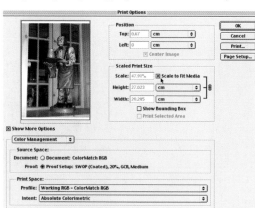

position by keying in known
measurements. All done
with minimal loss of brain
cells!

Above: shows the default setting
and how the print will appear on
an A4 sheet. Left: click Fit to Page
to get a full image.
Below: Uncheck "centre" and key
in a size to print a custom size
and position on the page.

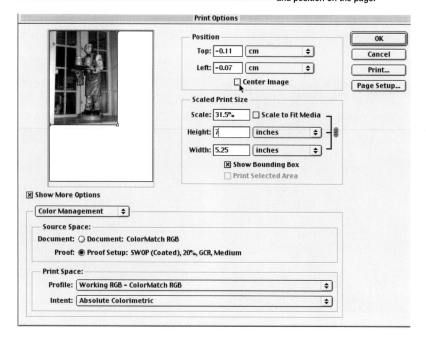

Print resolution

The number of dots along the length
and width of a print, measured in dots
per inch. Generally the more dots per
inch the higher the resolution. Most
inkjet printers print out at between
600dpi and 1440dpi but these are
slightly misleading as the figures allow
for between three and six ink colors that
are used to make up each dot.

A 1440dpi printer that uses six
individual ink colors actually means the
print resolution is more like 240dpi. The
highest true resolution is around 400dpi
for dye-sub printers and most books
and magazines print at around 300dpi.

This close-up of the tip of a Peacock butterfly's
wing shows how the dots make up the image.
This is the equivalent of a 1/4in area printed out
at 300dpi, so it shows the formation of around
75 dots across the length.

PSD

Photoshop's native format. Use this to save pictures when you want to keep the individual layers.

Profile to Profile

MENU	IMAGE ➔
	MODE ➔
	PROFILE TO PROFILE

Offers a wide range of profiles to convert the picture to suit the color space of the intended viewing monitor or printer output. Using this will change the colors on the working monitor and may make them look unreal.

If you select, say, RGB to Epson Color 600 using 720dpi PhotoPaper the image becomes lighter and ensures shadow detail is reproduced better.

Proof Setup

MENU	VIEW➔
	PROOF SETUP

Lets you view the image on the monitor as it will appear when reproduced on a specific output device. This is known as soft-proofing and saves you printing a hard copy of your document to preview how the colors will look.

Progressive JPEG

A file format used on the Web for quicker downloads. The image opens up progressively so you can get a rough idea what it looks like and either wait until it is at its highest resolution or click off and go elsewhere.

Purge command

This clears stuff out of the computer's memory such as the pattern held in the buffer ready for use by the Pattern Stamp tool.

You'd use the Purge command when the computer is starting to run slow or can't finish an action due to a lack of memory. Several options are available from the Purge drop down menu including Undo, Clipboard, Patterns, History.

Quadtones

Quadtones, like Duotones and Tritones, are grayscale images that use Process or Pantone colors to give a subtle color tone, almost like sepia, blue and gold toning of the conventional darkroom but with much more control and repeatability. Photoshop has a selection of preset Quadtones in the Duotone folder found in the Preset folder.

(See Duotones & Tritones)

From the preset selection, this adjusts the grayscale without adding a color hue and is used to ensure better printing in high quality books.

Another preset using Pantone colors to give a subtle green hue. This would be effective on still life shots but less so on a portrait.

One of the pantone presets that gives a slight sepia style glow.

A process colour preset that may work well with a vintage portrait.

Blue colors like this, created using the process color preset, can work well with glamour images.

A very subtle pantone preset that could lift a landscape. Would also work well with architectural images.

Quick Mask mode

Enter this mode by clicking on the icon near the bottom of the toolbar. It's a quick way to create a mask around a section. The mask can be increased using one of the Painting tools or decreased using the Eraser.

When you've made all your adjustments to the mask, click the off icon at the base of the toolbar and a selection will appear on the edges where the mask meets the unmasked area. Use the Paint or erase tool set to a small brush size to clean up rough areas.

r

RAM
Raster image
Rectangle tool
Rectangular Marquee tool
Replace Color
Resample Image
RGB
Rotate Canvas

Radial Blur
(See Blur modes)

Radial Fill
(See Gradient tool)

RAM

Short for Random Access Memory – the part of the computer that's used to run programs. Photoshop needs a minimum of 32Mb to run, 64Mb if it's going to be used for anything more than basic manipulation and as much as you can stick in to do complex multi-layer picture editing of large files.

Most computers can be upgraded and RAM, while fragile, is easy to install. You just take off the computer's side, back or lid, locate the memory slots and clip a stick of RAM into the hole. RAM used to be very expensive – a 32Mb chip cost around £900 a couple of years ago now it's around £1 per megabyte.

Could not open "Page 1.eps" because there is not enough memory (RAM).

OK

Raster image

Another name for a bitmap – image made up of a grid of pixels.

Rectangle tool

One of the vector based shapes that you draw on the page. The shape fills with the foreground colour and can be resized to suit the job you're doing. It appears on a new layer and has an adjustment icon where you can change its colour. These can also be used to mask individual image

Rectangle Tool	U
Rounded Rectangle Tool	U
Ellipse Tool	U
Polygon Tool	U
Line Tool	U
Custom Shape Tool	U

layers. The list also includes Rounded rectangle, Ellipse, Polygon, Line and Custom shape. Here a layer effect has been applied which then affects any shape that's added to the canvas.

Rectangular Marquee tool

A selection tool that puts a rectangular shaped marquee around the subject.

Rectangular Marquee Tool	M
Elliptical Marquee Tool	M
Single Row Marquee Tool	
Single Column Marquee Tool	

This can then be cut and pasted to somewhere else or edited.

Replace Color

MENU **IMAGE →**
 ADJUST →
 REPLACE COLOR

Use this mode to select and change the color of your subject. The palette that appears has a fuzziness scale that works like the tolerance setting – the higher it's set the more pixels are selected around the original color. This mode is useful when the subject you want to change has a strong color dominance as it's easier to select the area you want. Set the preview window to Selection and click on either the preview image or the main image using the Eye-dropper tool to select the color you want to change.

The preview image shows the color selected as white and the surrounding areas as black. You can then adjust the Hue, Saturation and Lightness. Use the +/- Eye-droppers to add to, or remove from, the color selected.

Resolution
(See Image Resolution)

RGB

Mode used to display colors on a computer monitor – R being Red, G green and B blue. The colors are mixed together in various proportions and intensities to create most of the visible spectrum with over 16.7 million colors.

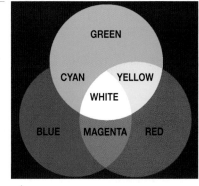

Photoshop assigns an intensity value to each pixel ranging from 0 (black) to 255 (white) for each of the RGB colors. Cyan, Magenta and Yellow are produced when different proportions of color overlap, for example R and G values of 255 mixed with a B value of 0 results in 100% Yellow.

Grey is created when there's an equal amount of R, G and B. When all the values are 255, the result is pure white and when the values are 0, pure black. This is known as additive color.

Ripple filter
(See Distort filters)

Resample Image

MENU **IMAGE →**
 IMAGE SIZE

If you want to make a picture smaller for use on a Web page, or bigger to enlarge for the wall, you have to take away or add pixels – known as resampling. The Image Size palette lets you change the image using the pixel dimension or measurements. Make sure Resample Image is checked.

(See Image size and Interpolation)

Rotate Canvas

MENU **IMAGE →**
 ROTATE CANVAS

Images scanned in can often appear the wrong way up or back to front. This option lets you rotate the canvas by 90° clockwise or anti-clockwise, 180° or flip horizontally or vertically.

If you take a photo with a wonky horizon you can adjust by slightly rotating the whole picture. Select Arbitary from the Rotate Canvas menu and key in the amount of rotation required in degrees.

You can also use the Transform option Edit→Transform→Rotate to rotate a selection or whole selected layer. Use the Grid option View→Show Grid to help align the horizontal or vertical elements.

S

Saturation

MENU	IMAGE ➜
	ADJUST ➜
	HUE/SATURATION
QUICK KEYS	CTRL+U

A slider control to adjust the colors in the image from –100 to +100. Dragging the slider to the left decreases the color in the image which is useful if you want a pastel effect or black & white.

Dragging to the right is the recipe for vivid colors – go too far and the image will look unnatural.

Saturation reduced to –100 knocks out all the color.

Increase to +100 and the colors become unreal.

Saving

MENU	FILE ➔	Saves the current
	SAVE	version over the
QUICK KEY	CTRL+S	original. If you prefer

to keep the original and have a different file for the new adjusted image select File➔Save As (Shift+Ctrl+S) and change the name. To make things easy just add 2 at the end of the current name so you know it's version two.

The Save As option also lets you change the file format.

(See individual file formats entries)

Save for Web

MENU	FILE ➔	One for Web
	SAVE FOR WEB	designers that was

introduced in Version 5.5. Open a picture you want to convert for the Web and when you've done all your retouching or enhancing go to Save for Web.

This brings up a palette to the side of your picture with a range of options to reduce the file size by resampling, file change and color reduction.

If you're not sure what effect various options will have on your image you can split the screen into two or four versions and apply a different setting to each.

The base of each picture has details of the new reduced file size and, very important for Web, the download time on a 56.6Kbps modem.

GIF
79.12K
15 sec @ 56.6Kbps

The Save for Web palette has options to vary the amount of lossy compression, as well as save the image in four different formats. The color palette can be reduced or optimized and the physical dimensions can be changed. Spend time with this mode and your Web images will fly.

Scale command
(See Transform)

Scratch disk

When your computer lacks the RAM needed to perform a complicated Photoshop task, the program uses its own virtual memory system known as a Scratch disk.

The Scratch disk is best assigned to the hard drive – removable drives are not recommended for this type of use. If you have partitioned your hard drive use a separate partition to hold the Scratch disk to the one that's running Photoshop for the best performance.

Selecting

When you want to edit part of an image it has to be selected. A selection can be made using several Photoshop tools such as the Lasso and Pen tools, Pens, Marquees, Magic Wand and Color Range. These are all explained in their relevant sections. The selection appears with a moving dotted line border that's often described as marching ants. Select➔All puts the marching ants around the whole image.

S

Selective color

MENU **IMAGE** →
    ADJUST
    SELECTIVE COLOR

Use this color correction mode to remove a color cast.

The palette has a drop down menu of the six additive and subtractive primary colors along with blacks, neutrals and whites. Select which you want to modify and then adjust the Cyan, Magenta, Yellow or Black content.

Adjusting the cyan slider in the red does not affect the cyan in any of the other areas. For color casts it's often just a case of nipping into the Neutral colors and adjusting the four sliders until the image looks balanced on screen.

You also need to choose between Relative and Absolute adjustment methods. With Relative selected you adjust the cyan, magenta, yellow and black sliders by a percentage of the total. A 25% magenta pixel becomes 30% when you add 20% (20% of 25% = 5%). Add 20% using the Absolute method and a 25% magenta becomes 45% magenta.

Sketch filters

MENU   **FILE**→
        SKETCH

A selection of filters that add hand-drawn texture to your images using the foreground and background colors.

The image becomes two tone but you could always use the History Brush to bring some more color back.

Sharpening
(See Unsharp Mask)

BAS RELIEF
Changes dark areas to the foreground color and light areas to the background color. Two sliders control the detail and smoothness of the effect.

Tip

● Set Detail at maximum and Smoothness at minimum for the kind of bas relief you'd create in a darkroom, especially when foreground and background colors are set to black & white.

CHROME
Produces an image with smooth edges and a variety of grey tones, making it look like highly reflective chrome.

Tips

● Images can look dull when this filter has been used. Adjust Levels to add contrast to the image.
● Doesn't work well with all subjects – go for bigger subjects with less detail.

CHARCOAL
Similar effect to Chalk & Charcoal. The foreground color is sketched on top of the background color.

CHALK & CHARCOAL
Recreates the image with solid mid-grey highlights and midtones.

The background becomes coarse chalk using the foreground color, and shadow areas are replaced with diagonal charcoal lines using the background color. Sliders control the balance of Chalk and Charcoal and the Stroke length.

CONTÉ CRAYON
Uses the foreground color for dark areas and the background color for light areas to supposedly recreate the effect of a Conté Crayon drawing – it's more like a tapestry effect.

Sliding controls let you adjust the strength of the foreground and background colors along with the Texture, Scaling, Relief and Light direction of the effect.

GRAPHIC PEN
Changes the image to a series of fine ink strokes which ensures detail of the original is still present. The foreground color is used for the pen's ink and the canvas becomes the background color.

Controls allow stroke length and direction to be adjusted along with the pen and paper color balance.

HALFTONE PATTERN
Produces a circle, dot or line pattern using the foreground and background colors.

NOTE PAPER
I can't see the point of this one! Controls let you adjust the proportions of the foreground and background colors, add grain and adjust the relief of the texture. Try a few settings then give up!

RETICULATION
Use the Density, Black and White sliders to control the reticulation effect that you'd normally only achieve by accident in the darkroom.

STAMP
Lightness/darkness and smoothness controls are all that are available for use with this potato-printing filter. Another one to avoid!

PHOTOCOPY
Another pointless effect that is supposed to turn the image into a photocopied effect. One of the filter's creators is obviously using a vintage photocopier!

PLASTER
Creates a slight 3D effect that looks like spilt fluid on a glass sheet. Dark areas are raised and light areas sink, unless you select Invert to reverse the effect.

TORN EDGES
One of the better Sketch filters that simulates a ragged paper effect. Best results are achieved by setting the Image balance slide midway; the smoothness to around 4 and the contrast to 1.

WATER PAPER
Makes the foreground and background colors flow into the image just as water color paint or ink would when applied to blotting paper.

Tip

● Use the Filter→Fade… command and try different Blend modes at different opacities to mix the background image with the effect you've just applied. Here Chalk & Charcoal has been blended with Soft Light mode.

S

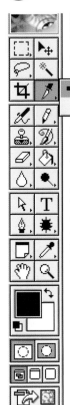

Slice Tool

The slice tool lets you cut a picture up ready for use

■ ⬏ Slice Tool	K
⬐ Slice Select Tool	K

on the Web. The overall picture will still appear seamless but each slice has its own Web code and can be adjusted so that it appears to change color, dim down, glow or whatever other effect you apply when the cursor goes over it.

Smart Blur
(See Blur modes)

Smudge tool

Click on the finger icon that's shared by the Sharpen & Blur tools in the toolbox and use it to push or smudge color from pixels into neighbouring pixels. It creates an effect like rubbing your finger through wet paint and, as with all paint tools, you can select the size of your fingertip.

⬤ Blur Tool	R
△ Sharpen Tool	R
■ ⬗ Smudge Tool	R

The Smudge tool can also be used to remove blemishes and spots by rubbing around the area to blend the dust spot with its surroundings.

The Smudge tool's options palette allows the Blending mode and pressure to be adjusted and it picks up the color under the pointer to paint, unless you select the Finger Painting option which uses the foreground color. Change to Finger Painting by pressing Alt (Windows) or Option (Mac OS) as you drag with the Smudge tool.

Selecting All Layers makes the Smudge tool use color from all the visible layers. When deselected it uses colors from just the active layer. You can also choose Size or Pressure when a pressure-sensitive drawing tablet is connected. These are greyed out when not available.

The Smudge tool can also be used to blur objects by rubbing over the surface in all directions. The effect can look like water's dripped onto a water color painting.

Snapshot

Lets you make a Snapshot (temporary copy) at any stage in the editing process. The snapshot appears in a list at the top of the History pallete and can be recalled by clicking on the Snapshot you want to return to.

You can make as many snapshots as you need to compare editing stages, return to certain states or compare two or more final techniques.

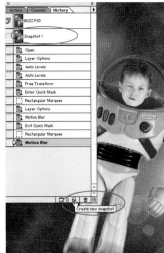

S

Soft light mode
(See Blending modes)

Solarizing
(See Stylize filter)

Spherize filter
(See Distort filters)

Sponge tool

Shares a place with the Dodge & Burn tools in the toolbox. The icon looks like a sponge and when dragged over the image surface either increases localized saturation or decreases saturation depending on which you selected from the Options palettte.

Stroke

MENU   FILE → STROKE

Used to place a border around a selection using either foreground or background color pixels. You can choose the width of the border, the position from the selection, Blend mode and the opacity. Version 6 has the color selector within the palette rather than you having to go to the foreground color in the toolbar to choose it.

Spot Color channels

Allows you to add and print a color that would normally not be possible from the normal CMYK gamut. You select the color using Pantone reference in a special Spot Color channel.

Select New Spot Channel from the Channels drop down menu and click on the color square to call up the color picker. Ignore the Out of Gamut warning and pick that lush fluro green or pink for the vivid heading or background. Selecting 100% solidity simulates a metallic color while 0% is more like a clear varnish effect.

Tip
● The Spot Color option works best when you have the image printed with a fifth color ink. Desktop printers use CMYK so you need to add the color to the normal channels Merge Spot Channel. The printer will then simulate the color using CMYK, but it may not be as vivid.

Tips
● As with all border creating methods, avoid colors that clash and distract from the subject.
● Use the Stroke command when you want to highlight part of a picture. Draw a circle round it using the Circular Marquee and apply a two or three pixel stroke in an eye-catching color.

S

Stylize filter

MENU   **FILTER →**
         STYLIZE →
Use these filters to create impressionist effects.

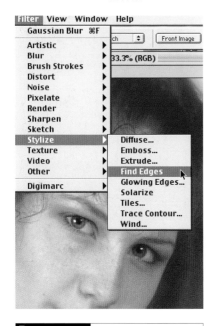

DIFFUSE

Shuffles pixels around randomly to create a soft, ragged looking image. Darken Only replaces light pixels with darker pixels. Lighten Only replaces dark pixels with lighter pixels.

EXTRUDE

Produces a 3D building block or pyramid effect. The height and size of blocks can be adjusted.

Tip

● Try applying the Pyramid Extrude after the block. Use small pixel values for the most detailed effect.

Tip

● Select Solid Front Faces to fill the front of each block with the average color. Keep it deselected to fill the front with the image.

EMBOSS

Locates high contrast edges and adds light and dark pixels to emphasize these edges. The strength of relief is increased using the Amount slider and the Height slider increases the 3D effect by making the image appear raised from its background. You can also adjust the angle that the embossing takes effect through 360°.

Tip

● Use the Fade command Filter→Fade Emboss Shift+Ctrl+F after applying the Emboss filter to bring back some color and detail. This example was set to Darken Blend too.

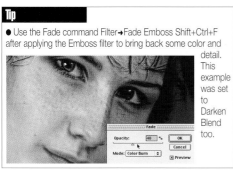

FIND EDGES

Emphasizes edges of a subject by detecting areas with high contrast edges and turning them black, while areas with low contrast appear white and medium contrast go grey.

Tip

● Selecting Image→Adjust→ Invert makes this look like the Glowing Edges effect.

S

Stylize filter
(cont.)

GLOWING EDGES
Opposite effect of Find Edges which makes the white edges that replace high contrast areas appear with a neon glow.

Tip

● Selecting Image→ Adjust→Invert makes this look like the Find Edges effect.

SOLARIZE
Produces an image like the photographic technique popularized by the likes of surrealist Man Ray who exposed prints briefly to light during development to fog and turn the highlights to black. Yuk!

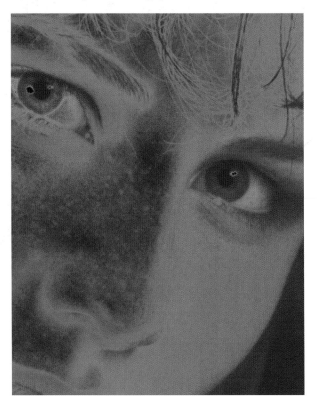

TILES
Makes the image break up into a series of tiles. You can select tile size, gaps between the tiles and the color of gaps between the tiles.

Tip

● Re apply the tile filter on an already tiled photo and select a larger maximum offset, then go to Edit>Fade and select overlay blend mode set to about 50% for a crazy effect.

123

TRACE CONTOUR
Creates thin outlines that vary in color around high contrast edges.

WIND
Imitates an unrealistic wind effect by producing streaks from the pixels. Three options include Wind, Blast and Stagger that can be applied coming either from the left or right.

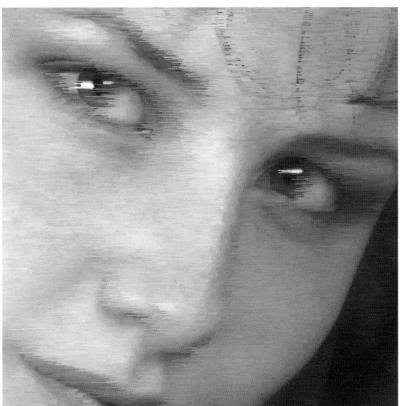

t

abcdefghijklmnopqrs**t**uvwxyz

Texture filters

MENU   FILTER ➜   A series of
         TEXTURE ➜   filters that
gives the image a textured appearance as though it has been ironed onto a textured surface.

CRAQUELURE
Produces a fine patch of cracks that looks a little like flaking paint. Choose your image carefully!

GRAIN
Adds grain to an image making it look more like a traditional photograph. This is a useful mode to apply to make a digital camera image blend with a traditional shot and look more natural when combined. There's a choice of grain types and the intensity and contrast can be controlled.

MOSAIC TILES

Breaks the image up into tiles separated by grout. The size of tiles can be adjusted along with the width and contrast of the grout.

PATCHWORK

Changes the image into a grid of colored squares. The colors produced are an average of all the enclosed pixels of each particular square. The size of grid can be changed and they appear in varying depths to simulate a very realistic looking patchwork.

STAINED GLASS

Draws a series of irregular shaped cells over the image, outlined by the foreground color, and fills them with an average of the contained pixels. The cell and border size can be changed.

TEXTURIZER

Adds a texture to the image making it look like it's printed on canvas.

TIFF format (Tagged-Image File Format)

A versatile format that can easily be read by Macs and PCs using a variety of software programs. It supports CMYK, RGB, and grayscale files with Alpha channels plus Lab, indexed-color and Bitmaps without Alpha channels. TIFF files can be compressed, without any loss in quality, using the LZW method to gain storage space, but they'll be slower to open and save.

Tiles filter
(See Stylize filters)

Tolerance settings
(See Magic Wand)

Tritone
(See Duotones)

t

Threshold mode

MENU   IMAGE ➔

        ADJUST ➔

        THRESHOLD

Makes a normal grayscale or color image appear like a high contrast lith image by discarding all tones including greys and leaving just black and white.

You can control where the black and white crossover points are using a slider on the Histogram.

Tolerance setting

Found in the Magic Wand options. It's used to adjust the number of pixel color variation selected from the one the magic wand touches. If the tolerance setting is high more pixel colors will be selected. If it's low fewer will be selected. Trial and error will help you determine what to set this to.

Tips

● Start small and work up or start big and work down until the wand is selecting more or less the area you want it to. Then adjust the tolerance to minimal setting and pick up wanted areas using the wand with the Alt key held down or remove parts of the selection with the wand and the Command key held down.

Toolbox

The area on the desktop where all the tools are located. Ones with arrows have pull-out sections with a choice of alternative tools.

Most of the toolbox icons can be double clicked to bring up the palette options box.

The bottom two icons appeared first with Photoshop 5.5 and allow easy transfer from Photoshop to Image Ready and back.

Shortcut keys are given throughout this book on the separate entries for toolbar contents.
(See Appendix C)

Transform

MENU   EDIT →   A series of options
TRANSFORM → that lets you change
the size, shape, and perspective of a
selection as well as rotate and flip it
either manually or numerically.

The selection appears with squares, or
handles, in the corners that you drag to
change the dimensions. It's ideal for
resizing an object when it's copied and
pasted into another image. You can also
use it to stretch landscapes and give
them a panoramic feel.

The area you want to change must
first be selected before you can use
these modes.

Tip
● When making the image grow out of the canvas
area increase the canvas beforehand to allow the
new 'stretched' area to appear.

Take any ordinary landscape and
stretch it using Transform→Scale
to create a panoramic print.

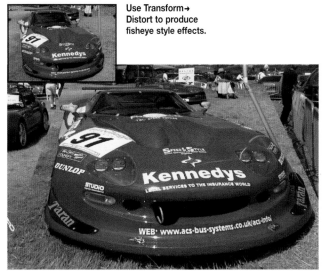

Use Transform→
Distort to produce
fisheye style effects.

Above: Copy and resize your subject using Transform→Scale to
create a realistic looking perspective.

Transform Again

Remembers that last Transform that you applied and
repeats the action. This is a useful option if you're
creating a composite picture and are pasting in and
adjusting several elements.

128

Transparent layer

A layer with areas that contain no pixels, such as a new Layer, appears with a chequered pattern. Any subsequent layers that are merged will only be affected by the non-transparent areas.

These are only available in the Photoshop PSD format and need to be merged if saved as TIFFs or JPEGs. Transparent areas are then replaced by white. Cut-outs can be saved by converting to clipping paths which prevent the white background appearing on the document.

Transparency masks

Use the Gradient Editor with the Transparency option selected to create a transparency mask. This can be used to help blend two layers or add a graduated filter effect to an image.

Trapping

MENU   IMAGE →
            TRAP
Produces an overlap on colors by the amount of pixels you key in. The overlap prevents gaps appearing between CMYK colors if there's a slight misalignment or movement of the printing plates. This technique is known as trapping and your printer will tell you if it's needed and what values to enter in the Trap dialogue box.

TWAIN

Would you believe this is short for Technology Without An Interesting Name! It's true. Basically it's a file that comes with scanners that you place in the Preferences folder on your Mac or the TWAIN folder of the Windows Directory on a PC. When you want to scan from within Photoshop you go to File→Import→TWAIN Acquire. If you have more than one scanner installed you first have to select the one you want, File→Import→Select TWAIN Source.

The benefit is you can keep within Photoshop while scanning pictures. Once the scan is complete the image appears in a new Photoshop document named Untitled. Save the scan straightaway, because if the computer crashes you'll lose the file and will have to scan again.

Photoshop 5.5 & 6.0 offer four Anti-alias options, rather than on or off that you have in Photoshop 5's palette. The options now include None (off), Crisp, Strong and Smooth from the pull down menu. To indicate what difference you would see on text I've magnified the top right of a letter S.

Type tool

Photoshop 6.0's Type tool continues to improve making it even easier for designers to create stunning text treatments. As well as being able to call from the system's usual font size, color and styles you can create type with selection borders using the Type Mask tool and fill with images or textures. Version 6.0 offers vector based type that you can increase in size without any jaggedness. This also offers more control so you can distort and bend the text alone or around objects.

Inner bevel gives a more defined style to text, especially when using black & white shading.

The Layer style palette has many options to change the look of the type. Here I've selected pillar Emboss using yellow and blue shading.

Type can now be bent and shaped in any direction and then you can add a style (right).

Undo

MENU	EDIT →
	UNDO
QUICK KEYS	CTRL+Z

If you don't like the effect of a filter you've just applied, or you've gone wrong with a brushstroke you can use Undo to take you back one step. Edit→StepForward/Step Backwards makes life even easier. It's like the History palette but uses shortcut keys to speed things up. Whatever you do can be simply undone.
(For multiple undos see History palette)

Tip
● Use Undo to revert to a previous setting when making adjustments to palette settings that have several options.

Use all Layers

Select this mode in the Rubber Stamp, Paint bucket or Sharpness/Blur/ Smudge palettes to ensure the color of all layers are merged to affect the active layer when the effect is applied. When Use all Layers is not selected only the colors in the active layer are sampled, cloned or smudged.

To show how Use all Layers mode works I used the Clone tool on this three layer image. A sample was taken from the letter R, but the streaky background layer was active. I then cloned across the image below the text resulting in just the one layer cloned. Doing the same with the Use all Layers box checked shows it picks up the word 'bear', the streaky background and the teddy making the cloning more interesting.

Unsharp Mask

MENU   FILTER →   A filter used to sharpen edges in an image and
          SHARPEN →   reduce blurring caused at the photographic,
          UNSHARP MASK   scanning, resampling, or printing stage. Unsharp
Mask locates pixels that differ from neighbouring pixels and increases their
contrast.

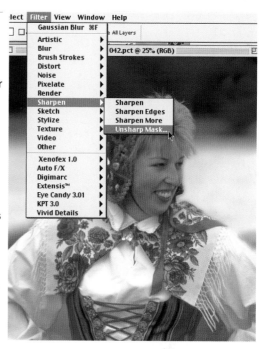

The dialogue box has Amount, Radius and Threshold settings that are
adjusted by either dragging sliders or manually entering values.

Amount changes the pixel contrast by the amount you set. When
producing images for on-screen viewing you can judge the effect quite
accurately and a setting of 50-100% is fine, but for printed output it's not
as easy. Try a setting of between 150% and 200%.

Radius controls the number of pixels surrounding the edge pixels that
will be affected by sharpening. A lower value sharpens just the edge pixels
while a higher value sharpens a wider band of pixels. The amount you set
also depends on the size of the image – use a smaller number for a lower
resolution image and increase the number for a higher resolution image.
Go too high and the edges will become too contrasty.

Threshold, set at a default of 0, sharpens all the pixels. Moving the slider
upwards prevents the filter from affecting pixels that are similar to
neighbouring pixels. A value of between 2 and 20 is a good starting point.
The higher you go the less effect Unsharp Mask will have on the image.

Above left: Apply too
much Unsharp Mask
and the picture will
become too harsh
caused by overly
sharp edge detail.
Above: Adjusting the
setting to around
120% improves the
result.

Tips

● Bright colors can become overly saturated when
Unsharp Mask has been applied and dust marks are
easily enhanced. Try converting the image to Lab
mode and apply the filter to the Lightness channel
only to sharpen the image without affecting the color.
● Run Unsharp Mask twice at half the single settings
for a more subtle effect.

V-Z

Variations

MENU **IMAGE →**
      ADJUST →
      VARIATIONS

This color balance control, that also lets you adjust image contrast and brightness, is the most colorful window of all the Photoshop dialogue boxes with its series of preview images.

The original selection and the adjusted selection appear at the top.

The menu appears at their side and from here you select Shadows, Midtones, or Highlights to adjust dark, middle or light areas.

Set the Fine/ Coarse slider to control the amount of adjustment.

Seven pictures appear with the current example in the centre and the color options around the edges.
To add a color to the image, click the appropriate color image and to subtract a color, click the image on the opposite side.

These three preview images are used to adjust image brightness. The centre is the current version, the one above makes the centre lighter and the one below makes it darker.

Whoops

● If the Variations command is missing from the Adjust submenu check that the Variations plug-in module has been installed.

Above left: A coarse setting shows extreme colour changes. Above right: Turn Show Clipping on to display a neon preview of areas in the image that have become pure white or pure black as a result of your adjustments

Saturation varies the result from vivid color to monotone.

Web colors

When using pictures on the Web there are a limited number of colors that can be selected when writing HTML code. Photoshop 5.5 and 6.0 lets you select the Web palette from the Color Picker and when you pick a color, the HTML reference code appears for the selected color. The blue color I picked below has an HTML code of 663399.

Watercolor filter
(See Artistic filters)

Watermarks

MENU   FILTER →
         DIGIMARC
         EMBED WATERMARK

Adding a watermark to your image is a safe way of protecting the copyright. Digimarc embeds a digital watermark to the image. It's imperceptible to the human eye but is durable in digital and printed forms and will survive typical image edits and file format conversions. A © symbol appears by the title to warn any viewers that the copyright should be respected. To use this feature you have to register with Digimarc and receive a special ID number.

Wet edges

An option in the Brush palette that produces a brushstroke with a build-up of color on the edges to simulate a watercolor paintbrush effect.

Web Photo Gallery

MENU FILE →
      AUTOMATE →
    WEB PHOTO GALLERY

It's never been easier to get your pictures on-line with this new feature introduced in Photoshop version 5.5. This auto mode converts your pictures into Web manageable sizes, then writes some HTML code so that they appear as thumbnails on an opening index page. Clicking on an individual picture brings up a full screen version. The code includes arrows to navigate backwards or forwards through the gallery.

All the HTML pages, pictures and thumbnails are stored in the destination folder.

Various menu options let you set up this feature so that it creates the ideal Web page and style for you. You can select the number of images shown per page, the layout, text color and size, along with image quality, destination folder and even add links.

Opening up the main page gives a thumbnail index of all the pictures on the site.

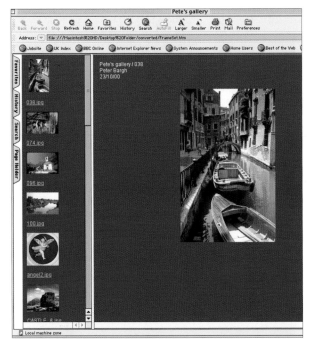

The palette has options to generate the pictures at various sizes. The site will work quicker when small files are selected, but image quality will be poorer.

Click on a thumbnail to bring up a single image on a page. The arrows on the top are used to navigate through the pictures or return to the main page.

ZigZag filter
(See Distort filters)

Zoom tool

QUICK KEYS   SHIFT+Z

Used to magnify or reduce the image on screen. The zoom options palette has one choice – resize windows to fit. When selected the window grows or contracts with the image.

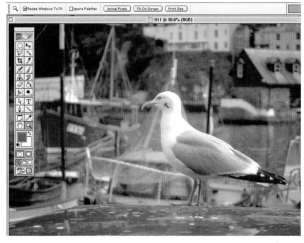

When PC users click on the right-hand mouse key with the Zoom tool selected they're greeted with a new menu to fit to screen, view at 100% or print size. You can also select zoom in and zoom out from here. If you hold the Alt key down

and click on the mouse the image will zoom out. **(See Navigator palette)**

Zoom set to 237%.

Zoom set to maximum 1600%.

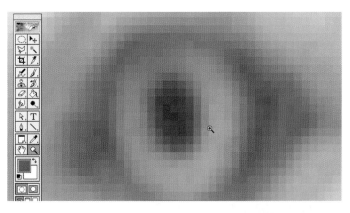

Tips

● You don't have to call up the Zoom tool to change magnification. Go to the image size box in the bottom left corner of your picture and manually key in a percentage to change the size.

● Click and hold down the mouse at the top left of the area you want to magnify and drag to the bottom right. The image will then magnify to include just the selected area.

Index

Appendix A: Photoshop versions compared

Every time Adobe update Photoshop, users ask whether it's worth upgrading. Often there are only a few changes, but they're usually 'must haves', making it hard not to want to upgrade. Throughout this book I've illustrated features that come with Photoshop 5.5 or 6.0. If you have an earlier version or a light edition (LE), use this chart to see whether the feature is available on your copy.

Photoshop feature changes	v3.0	v4.0	v5.0	LE	v5.5	v6.0
Color support						
CMYK, Lab, Duotone and Multichannel	☺	☺	☺		☺	☺
Color management and colour sample			☺		☺	☺
Color separations	☺	☺	☺		☺	☺
RGB, Indexed Color and Grayscale	☺	☺	☺	☺	☺	☺
Compatibility						
CMYK, Illustrator, PostScript and Acrobat Import	☺	☺	☺		☺	☺
Exports paths to Illustrator	☺	☺	☺		☺	☺
Print preview and soft proofing						☺
Creative features						
3D Transform plug-in			☺		☺	☺
Adjustment Layers		☺	☺		☺	☺
Annotation tools						☺
Art History Brush					☺	☺
Auto editing using the Actions palette		☺	☺		☺	☺
Auto Shadow, Bevel, Glow			☺		☺	☺
Background & Magic Eraser					☺	☺
Batch processing		☺	☺		☺	☺
Channel editing			☺		☺	☺
Color correction controls	☺	☺	☺	☺	☺	☺
Color Range command	☺	☺	☺		☺	☺
Contact sheet			☺		☺	☺
Crop tool with transform feature						☺
Digital Watermark		☺	☺		☺	☺
Extract Image command					☺	☺
Guides & Grids for precise alignment		☺	☺		☺	☺
History palette for multiple undo			☺		☺	☺
Layers	☺	☺	☺	☺	☺	☺
Layer alignment and layer effects			☺		☺	☺
Layer sets						☺
Layer styles						☺
Measuring tool			☺		☺	☺
Magnetic Lasso			☺	☺	☺	☺
Magnetic Pen			☺		☺	☺
Navigator		☺	☺	☺	☺	☺
Number of special effects filters	42+	90+		95+	95+	95+
Painting tools	☺	☺	☺	☺	☺	☺
Paths	☺	☺	☺		☺	☺
Retouching tools	☺	☺	☺	☺	☺	☺
Spot color channels			☺		☺	☺
Text tools	☺	☺	☺	☺	☺	☺
Vector shape and text support						☺
Web support						
Import/export GIF, JPEG and PNG files				☺	☺	☺
Image Ready™					v2.0	v3.0
Image slicing					☺	☺
Web palette			☺	☺	☺	☺

Appendix B: Typefaces

Your computer will, no doubt, come preloaded with a selection of typefaces, known as fonts. These can be accessed from Photoshop's Type tool and used in a number of ways with your images.

One option is to make postcards or greetings cards and use the type as the main message. You could also use the type to caption pictures, or as a supplement to a creative image, faded back as a layer.

The main thing to consider is the font you use. A modern face used on a sepia toned collage will look out of place. This book is created using Helvetica Neue and here's a selection of other fonts that you're likely to have access to. They are all set in 12 point. Select with care!

Two of the safest fonts to use on the Web are Arial and Verdana because all PC and Mac computers will have these two installed.

Photoshop A to Z in Apple Chancery

Photoshop A to Z in Arial

PHOTOSHOP A TO Z IN BALLOON D

Photoshop A to Z in Baskerville

Photoshop A to Z in Bauhaus 93

Photoshop A to Z in Bell MT

Photoshop A to Z in Book Antiqua

Photoshop A to Z in Bookman Old

Photoshop A to Z in Britannic Bold

Photoshop A to Z in Brush Script MT

Photoshop A to Z in Calisto MT

PHOTOSHOP A TO Z IN CAPITAL REG

Photoshop A to Z in Century Gothic

Photoshop A to Z in Century Schoolbook

Photoshop A to Z in Charcoal

Photoshop A to Z in Chicago

Photoshop A to Z in Comic Sans

Photoshop A to Z in Cooper Black

PHOTOSHOP A TO Z IN COPPER PLATE

PHOTOSHOP A TO Z IN CUTOUT

Photoshop A to Z in Courier

PHOTOSHOP A TO Z IN DESDEMONA

Photoshop A to Z in Edwardian Script

Photoshop A to Z in Eurostile

Photoshop A to Z in Folio T

Photoshop A to Z in Footlight

Photoshop A to Z in Futura Light

Photoshop A to Z in Gadget regular

Photoshop A to Z in Garamond

Photoshop A to Z in Geneva

Photoshop A to Z in Georgia

Photoshop A to Z in Giddyup

Photoshop A to Z in Gill Sans

Photoshop A to Z in Gloucester

Photoshop A to Z in Goudy Old Style

Photoshop A to Z in Harrington

Photoshop A to Z in Helvetica

Photoshop A to Z in Helvetica Neue 65

Photoshop A to Z in Impact

Photoshop A to Z in Imprint

Photoshop A to Z in Kino MT

Photoshop A to Z in Letter Gothic

Photoshop A to Z in Lucinda Blackletter

Photoshop A to Z in Lucinda Bright

Photoshop A to Z in Lydian

Photoshop A to Z in Matura Script

Photoshop A to Z in Micrograma

Photoshop A to Z in Minion Web

Photoshop A to Z in Mistral

Photoshop A to Z in Modern

PHOTOSHOP A TO Z IN MOJO

Photoshop A to Z in Monaco

Photoshop A to Z in Mono Corsiva

Photoshop A to Z in Myriad

Photoshop A to Z in New York

Photoshop A to Z in News Gothic

Photoshop A to Z in Onyx

PHOTOSHOP A TO Z IN OUCH

Photoshop A to Z in Palatino

Photoshop A to Z in Postino

Photoshop A to Z in Playbill

PHOTOSHOP A TO Z IN PERPETUA

Photoshop A to Z in Rockwell

Photoshop A to Z in Sand Regular

PHOTOSHOP A TO Z IN STENCIL

Photoshop A to Z in Tahoma

Photoshop A to Z in Techno

Photoshop A to Z in Teletext

Photoshop A to Z in Textile

Photoshop A to Z in Times

Photoshop A to Z in Trebuchet MS

Photoshop A to Z in Verdana

Appendix C: Useful shortcuts

TOOLBAR

All of the tools in Photoshop's toolbar can be accessed using shortcut keys. Hold down the Alt + shortcut key to scroll through multiple options.

Adobe online
Click here for a direct link to the Adobe Web site

Marquees: Shortcut key M
Use to select areas of an image

Move tool: Shortcut key V
Use to move selection

Lasso: Shortcut key L
Use to select areas of pixels

Magic Wand: Shortcut key W
Use to select pixels

Crop: Shortcut key C
Cuts out unwanted surroundings

Slice & Slice select: Shortcut key K
Use to paint color to an image

Airbrush: Shortcut key J
Use to paint color to an image

Pencil, Paintbrush: Shortcut key B
Use to draw sharp edged detail

Clone Stamp: Shortcut key S
Clones pixels from one area of an image to another

History & Art History Brush: Shortcut key K
Paints from a previous History state

Eraser: Shortcut key E
Use to rub out selected pixels

Paint bucket, Gradient: Shortcut key G
Use to fill an area with color

Blur, Sharpen, Smudge: Shortcut key R
Use to increase or decrease sharpness

Dodge, Burn Sponge: Shortcut key O
Use to increase or decrease exposure locally

Path Selection: Shortcut key A
Use to move paths or anchor points

Type tool: Shortcut key T
Use to add text to your pictures

Pen tool: Shortcut key P
Use to make smooth selections and paths

Line and Vector shapes: Shortcut key U
Use to add various shapes to your pictures

Notes and Audio Annotation: Shortcut key N
Use to add text or sound message to picture

Eye-dropper: Shortcut key I
Use to sample color from image

Hand: Shortcut key H
Moves the area being viewed on screen

Zoom: Shortcut key Z
Use to magnify or reduce image on screen

Foreground color: Shortcut key X
Switches between foreground and background colors

Background color: Shortcut key X
Switches between foreground and background colors

Default colors: Shortcut key D
Switches to black & white colors

Standard mode: Shortcut key Q
Switches between Standard and Quick Mask modes

Quick Mask mode: Shortcut key Q
Switches between Standard and Quick Mask modes

Screen mode: Shortcut key F
Switches between Standard screen (left), Full screen with menus (middle) and Full screen with no menus (right)

Program Link
Jump straight into Adobe Image Ready

BLEND MODES

All the Blend modes have shortcuts. Hold down the Shift key + Alt with the following letters:

PALETTES

Keeping your desktop clear of junk is essential for clean working, especially if you have a smaller monitor. Palettes are one of the biggest culprits for clogging up space. Fortunately F keys will open and close palettes with ease.

F5 shows or hides Brush palette on version 5.5 and before.

Info palette
F8 shows or hides it.

Color palette
F6 shows or hides it.

Actions palette
F9 shows or hides it.

Layers palette
F7 shows or hides it.

EXTRACT MODE

The Extract toolbox of Photoshop 5.5 has the following quick keys.

- B
- G
- E
- I
- C
- T
- Z
- H

IMAGE HANDLING

Open Image: Option(Mac)/Ctrl(PC)+O
New Canvas: Option(Mac)/Ctrl(PC)+N
Save Image: Option(Mac)/Ctrl(PC)+S
Close Image: Option(Mac)/Ctrl(PC)+W

Print Image: Option(Mac)/Ctrl(PC)+P

Undo: Option(Mac)/Ctrl(PC)+U
Cut: Option(Mac)/Ctrl(PC)+X
Copy: Option(Mac)/Ctrl(PC)+C
Paste: Option(Mac)/Ctrl(PC)+P

MOVING SELECTIONS

Use the Move tool and the up, down, left and right arrows to move the selection one pixel at a time.

Hold down the Shift key when using the arrows to move the selection 10 pixels at a time.

PALETTE VIEWS

The Tab key shows or hides all palettes.

Shift + Tab key shows or hides all but the toolbox.

Appendix D: Preferences

Use these for setting up Photoshop to run just as you want it. The palette has several sub menus that can be scrolled down by using the up and down arrows. Before you first use Photoshop it's worth becoming familiar with the options and setting up the program to run smoother by turning off options you won't need. Got to the File menu and then Preferences and choose General to see the palette below.

General

When switched on, this transfers the clipboard contents to the system's clipboard when you switch programs and can slow you down.

Use this to scroll through the various preference palettes.

Useful if you're working on images where filters take ages to apply. You can go off and do something else and the program will call you when it has done its job.

Select the number of Actions that are held in the image's History palette.

Choice of Photoshop or Windows style interface.

Three options, but Bicubic is best.

Shows a preview of the color effect as you drag the slider.

Turn this on so that other programs can recognize the Pantone color's name when working with duotones.

Displays keyboard shortcuts and labels when you move your curser over a tool or palette option. Use these until you're familiar with the program's features.

Places palettes in their original positions on screen.

New to Photoshop 5.5, this mode ensures a file that's open in Photoshop is updated while you work on the same in Image Ready and vice versa.

Option to view Chinese, Japanese, and Korean (CJK) type.

Resets all warning messages that you've stopped from appearing by selecting the 'Don't Show Again' option.

Returns any tool settings that you've made back to their defaults.

When turned on you have to hold down the shift key and the quick key to change between options in the toolbar.

Views the English font name when CJK type is selected

Leave switched on to ensure display palettes and the toolbox appear in the same spot on screen even when you restart the program.

Preferences

General

Color Picker: Adobe

Interpolation: Bicubic (Better)

Redo Key: Cmd+Z (Toggles Undo/Redo)   History States: 20

OK
Cancel
Prev
Next

Options

☒ Export Clipboard
☐ Short PANTONE Names
☒ Show Tool Tips
☒ Keyboard Zoom Resizes Windows
☐ Auto-update open documents
☐ Show Asian Text Options

☑ Beep When Done
☒ Dynamic Color Sliders
☒ Save Palette Locations
☒ Show Font Names in English
☒ Use Shift Key for Tool Switch

Reset All Warning Dialogs

Reset All Tools

Automatically adds a three letter file description to the end of newly saved files so they can be read by Windows programs on a PC.

Ensures the file is fully compatible with earlier versions of Photoshop but it makes the file size larger.

Lists specified number of images previously worked on for quick recall from File→Open recent.

Never save: Saves files without previews. Always save: Saves files with previews. Ask when saving: Saves previews on individual file basis.

Use Lower Case adds a file extension using lower case characters (.jpg). When unchecked it adds one using upper case characters (.JPG).

Increases the speed that a histogram appears by producing it from the Cached sample. The preview won't be as good, though.

Increase this to work faster on large files, providing you have enough RAM available for it to run smoothly.

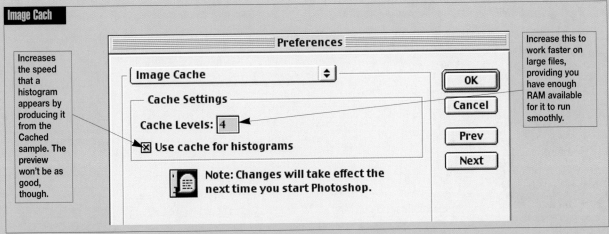

Change the measurement scale used on the ruler from this box.

Change the type measurements from points to pixels to mm.

Size images up to fit in the columns of a newspaper or magazine.

Appendix D: Preferences

Continued.

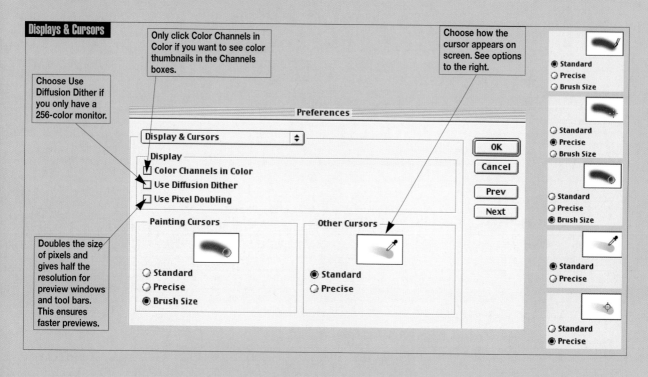

Displays & Cursors

Choose Use Diffusion Dither if you only have a 256-color monitor.

Only click Color Channels in Color if you want to see color thumbnails in the Channels boxes.

Choose how the cursor appears on screen. See options to the right.

Doubles the size of pixels and gives half the resolution for preview windows and tool bars. This ensures faster previews.

Preferences

Display & Cursors

Display
- ☑ Color Channels in Color
- ☐ Use Diffusion Dither
- ☐ Use Pixel Doubling

Painting Cursors
- ○ Standard
- ○ Precise
- ● Brush Size

Other Cursors
- ● Standard
- ○ Precise

OK
Cancel
Prev
Next

- ● Standard
- ○ Precise
- ○ Brush Size

- ○ Standard
- ● Precise
- ○ Brush Size

- ○ Standard
- ○ Precise
- ● Brush Size

- ● Standard
- ○ Precise

- ○ Standard
- ● Precise

Plug-Ins & Scratch Disk

Lets you choose an alternative plug-in folder or directory from the list for plug-ins and display its contents by double-clicking the folder.

WARNING: If you change the plug-ins location, the usual Photoshop plug-ins, filters and scanners will be unavailable until you change back to the Plug-Ins location inside the application folder.

Preferences

Plug-Ins & Scratch Disks

☒ Additional Plug-Ins Folder

Macintosh HD:programs: Adobe ® Photoshop ® 6.0:Plug-Ins:

Choose...

Scratch Disks

First: *Startup*

Second: *None*

Third: *None*

Fourth: *None*

Note: Scratch disks will remain in use until you quit Photoshop.

OK
Cancel
Prev
Next

You can assign up to four locations for Scratch disks to improve the speed that Photoshop works, but don't use removable storage, such as a Zip drive as a location.

Grid Colors lets you pick a grey pattern or a color.

The color and size of grid you select are displayed in the preview window

The transparent areas of a document appear as a checkerboard pattern that can be varied in size. Choose None and the transparent areas in the layer will appear white.

Use Video Alpha should only be checked if you have hardware with a chroma key facility.

Shows when colors in an RGB image won't print out correctly. Select a color by clicking on the square in this palette and any colors in your image that are out of the printer's gamut will appear covered with this warning color.

Preferences

Transparency & Gamut

OK

Cancel

Prev

Next

Transparency Settings

Grid Size: Medium

Grid Colors: Light

☐ Use video alpha (requires hardware support)

Gamut Warning

Color:

Opacity: 100 ▶ %

Pick a color for guides or the grid from the pre-selected range or from the Color palette. Choose one that will be seen above your images, such as bright yellow.

Choose straight lines or dashes for guides and grids.

Adjust the grid spacing by entering an amount in this box.

Enter an amount to subdivide the grid.

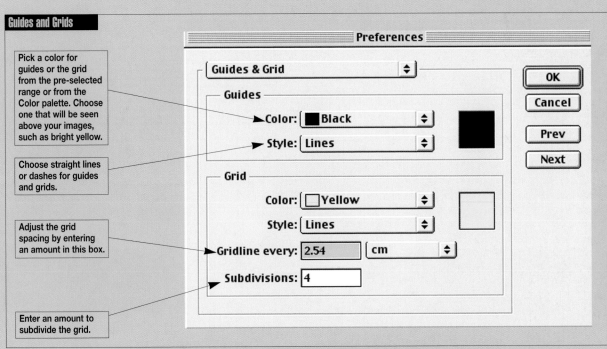

Preferences

Guides & Grid

OK

Cancel

Prev

Next

Guides

Color: Black

Style: Lines

Grid

Color: Yellow

Style: Lines

Gridline every: 2.54 cm

Subdivisions: 4

Appendix E: Useful Web sites

Adobe

<www.adobe.com/products/photoshop/main.html>

A slik design, as you'd expect from the masters of imaging software. Adobe's official site now requests that you key in the serial number of Photoshop to enter the new 'Expert' area. If you haven't registered your program it will first ask you to do so. This took me 15 minutes and then you can gain access to a stunning collection of material with galleries, downloads, articles from experts, tips pages and a user forum.

Photoshop Tutorials

<www.rice.edu/Computer/Tutorials/ravl/pshop//>

Superb site with loads of useful material based around Photoshop 3. The layout is visually very basic but if you need to know about file formats, importing, editing, manipulating or printing, take a trip through this fantastic site.

PC Resources for Photoshop

<showcase.netins.net/web/wolf359/plugcomm.htm>

Stunning, that's the only word needed to describe this site – a veritable bonanza of interesting goodies for Photoshop owners. Nicely designed and crammed with useful stuff, including 62 collections of filter effects by Andrew Buckle. Go here first.

Alien Skin

The makers of Photoshop plug-ins, Xenofex and Eye Candy, have this site where you can download trial versions, read about the features, see the effects the programs create or buy full versions. You can even visit the press lounge and read the latest news, often before it reaches the magazines.

Martin Evening

<www.evening.demon.co.uk>

Martin is a professional photographer and Photoshop user. The site offers free PDF downloads of several Photoshop tutorials and examples of his work shooting fashion models for London hairdressing salons. Great inspiration and beautiful models There's also a plug for his book *Adobe Photoshop 6.0 for Photographers*.

Boxtop Software

www.boxtopsoft.com/ProJPEG/index.html

Go here for a really fast and highly effective JPEG compressor. The plug-in can be downloaded from the site and costs $49.99. There are several other programs available for GIF compression and color optimization for the Web.

The Plug Page

<www.boxtopsoft.com/plugpage/>

Go here to find interesting plug-ins to download and expand the flexibility of Photoshop.

Photoshop org

Offers useful Photoshop tutorials, galleries, tools, job vacancies and links to other sites. When I visited there was an invite for you to redesign the site, which it needed. By the time you read this it's probably sorted.

Appendix E: Useful Web sites

Continued.

Planet Photoshop

<www.planetphotoshop.com>

A fast site to move around in, which is important when your time is precious. The menu items on the left call up loads of stuff on the right – great tutorials with lots of links and a mass of extremely useful tips, techniques and advice on all things Photoshop...lovely.

CoolType

<webdeveloper.com/design/>

If text is something you want to add to your pictures, go here for some, as the name suggests, cool effects. There are plenty of step-by-step techniques to help you improve the way text looks, including fire, bevels, charcoal and chalk.

Photoshop Plugged in

<perso.club-internet.fr/gpl/>

A collection of sites listed and rated for quality. The list includes 90 commercial sites and 66 freeware options. Each has a mark out of five for usefulness.

You can also download PDF tutorials, but be warned one of these took around 25 minutes on a standard 56Kbps modem, and it only had two pages.

A fantastic resource with individual entries for over 150 products and sites. The sad thing is it was last updated in winter 1999. Still useful for lots of links and ideas.

Mccannas.com

An odd site that offers loads of great tutorials, yet it looks like the designer of the site could do with reading a few of the tips. You are presented with a mish mash of styles, type faces and layouts but it's worth putting up with for the large supply of great material within.

Appendix E: Useful Web sites

Continued.

Ultimate Photoshop

First class site that's well designed, easy to navigate and well worth a visit. Has comprehensive step-by-step tutorials, a forum where you can ask questions about Photoshop and plenty of links to free plug-ins. There's even direct links to US retail outlets selling Photoshop and plug-ins. Sadly the owner has stopped developing it and gone to medical school!

Xaos tools

Another site run by a software maker who produces Paint Alchemy and Terrazzo. The site gives overviews of the plug-in programs with examples of work, trial downloads and upgrades.

Sapphire Innovations

A large collection of patterns and effects that can be used as background layers or text fills. Some are crazy style, some are more subtle... basically something for every taste. Most of the plug-ins are for PCs.

SAPPHIRE PATTERNS VOL 1 FOR PHOTOSHOP 6

Patterns for Photoshop 6.   Photoshop 6 - PC & Mac

A wide variety of styles and colours. 300+ patterns in all. 250 x 250 patterns. Royalty-free.

Patterns that can be used as layer effects or text fills

Patterns that can be used as brush effects

and more.

A really superb new add-on to Photoshop 6.

If you would like further info about this product please e-mail us,

PHOTOSHOP PLUGINS

PRODUCTS

Innovations Vol 1 (.5.2) - Photoshop ® Plugins.

DESCRIPTION

This product consists of 35 plugins for Photoshop ® 5+ and other applications that support the plugin format.

Includes the following plugins

Edge effects, OpArt effects, LiftOff effects, Wave opart effects, Wavey City, Rotate effects, emboss effects, Shudder, Colour effects, random colour effects, teethmark distortions, reflections, line effects, colour additions, wave distortions, cutting distortions and more. The new set also includes Inverse time, randomizer and a new 'gradient' plugin, colour flow.

The new plugins include some additional threshold effects, posterisation and blurring plugins, with simpler and easier to use interfaces.

Adobe Photoshop Web reference

<www.adscape.com/eyedesign/photoshop/>

A very useful reference site that has plenty of Photoshop info but only on versions 3 and 4. Fortunately many of the features are available on the latest releases so it's worth a visit. There's a good section on Actions, palettes, shortcuts and Layers. And the section on filters shows an image change to the effect you select as you click on the filter.

Filters: Distort: Diffuse Glow
- Graininess: 2
- Glow Amount: 10
- Clear Amount: 15

Intangible

<www.Intangible.org/Features/mcintyre/mcicontents.html>

I first came across Catherine's work when I was working on *Digital PhotoFX* magazine. Catherine sent in a portfolio of what I still think is some of the most beautiful images I've seen. The work combines the naked body with found objects on multiple Photoshop layers. Catherine has since gone on to produce a book and more superb work using old photographs, animal skeletons and such like. This site is a great introduction to her imagery with an extremely well presented layout.

Go here for inspiration.

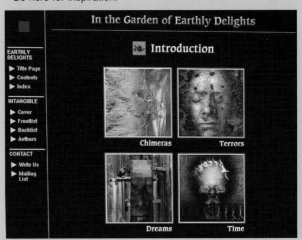

ePHOTOzine

<www.ephotozine.com>

I couldn't go without dropping a plug in for my own Web site. This one will suit photographers of all types. Digital photographers can pick up reviews of equipment, download Photoshop tutorials and check out the work of other digital-image makers. It's still in its development stages, but I plan to make it the ultimate photo resource centre.

Appendix F: Plug-in filters

A filter that offers additional features to the standard program. Photoshop supports third-party filters that can be added to the plug-ins folder to increase the program's flexibility. Many of the current supplied range used to be third-party options.

You can buy plug-ins such as Xaos Tools, Paint Alchemy, Kai's Power Tools, AutoFX Photo/Graphic Edges and Alien Skin's Eye Candy 4000. Others can be downloaded from the Web.

Auto F/X PhotoGraphic Edges is a useful plug-in that adds an edge to your image. The edges range from rough ragged effects to elaborate designs. Some emulate the edges that you'd get using Polaroid – a technique that's often used by fashion photographers.

Each edge can be edited to alter the depth, width, density, etc. Use this to give your pictures the edge – oh dear!

You can also create pattern effects with the latest packs from AutoF/X that have over 10,000 edges, borders, frames and patterns!

Kai's PowerTools is an amazing package of tricks from the man who invented Goo. One of the filters is a very flexible Gaussian Blur, used in this example to knock the castle out of focus.

First select the area you want out of focus in Photoshop. Add a large feather to avoid a harsh edge and call up the Gaussian Blur filter. The preview is quicker than Photoshop's too.

Kai's PowerTools has a few other gimmicks that are exciting the first time you discover them, but the novelty soon wears off.

Here the same picture was massacred twice using the Planar Tiling mode in Parquet tiling (right) and Planar tiling (below).

The Page Curl filter, from Kai's PhotoTools could be used for special effect in a presentation or brochure, but is a little too gimmicky for normal use.

The Noise mode of Kai's PhotoTools adds an interesting grainy feel to the image and could be used quite effectively on black & white too.

Appendix F: Plug-in filters

Continued.

Kai's PowerTools Texture Explorer is great for making backgrounds or sandwiching images with a funky texture.

Extensis PhotoTools brings a whole new range of tool bars to the page. You can select which to have on screen and from these, perform many of the Photoshop tasks that you'd normally have to go hunting for in the menu bars. Once you get used to the PhotoTools icons you can whizz through tasks.

Extensis PhotoTools has some great features for making shadows, buttons and textures for use on the Web or text illustrated images. You can also emboss, add glows and use the Gif Animator to make your Web pages come alive.

Above: Kai's PowerTools Twirl feature, set to Kaleidoscope mode, plays havoc with your images. Right: A useful test strip printer from Vivid Details shows various versions of the image that you can print out to determine color balance in as little as 1% increments.

Extensis Intellihance Pro is a powerful program with multi-window previews, right, to check for color accuracy and sharpness. Pre-set corrections can be saved and applied to images later.

Piccolo is not a plug-in, but it works alongside Photoshop. As well as being able to search through the contents of your computer's hard drive (PC only) and locate all the pictures, it also detects when a CD or memory card are inserted and automatically runs.

Any folders that hold pictures appear in a directory window with a green icon next to them. If you click on a folder containing images the pictures are previewed in slide frames. Clicking on one brings up the individual image which can then be edited.

The print feature lets you print multiple pictures on one A4 sheet and change the size and position within their areas on the sheet.

Vivid Details Test Strip is another program that's designed to make colour correction easier. This one lets you change the colour exposure and saturation, in varying increments, and view the results. You can also print out to check the effect your paper and printer will have. Use this for perfect results.

A Mac version of Piccolo is currently in development, but the Mac brigade can opt for the Shareware program QPict. It doesn't automatically detect a CD but by dragging a folder containing images over the QPICT icon you open up a slide sheet with all the pictures. Then click on one to magnify it. Like Piccolo you can print a contact sheet, but you can't resize pictures within the frames on QPict. It does have a very useful batch conversion process and can create Photoshop thumbnails.

Both QPict and Piccolo are great programs if you want to view the results quickly before taking the best into Photoshop for serious editing.

158

Appendix F: Plug-in filters

Continued.

Xenofex, from Alien Skin, is a useful addition to the vast filter range provided with Photoshop. It has a collection of 16 additional filter effects that can be applied to your images. The one I like most is Baked Earth which gives a dry mud cracked appearance to an image (below).

But others that can be put to good use include Lightning that adds forks of lightning to an image; Crumple to give a screwed up and reopened paper feel; and Flag that creates the wavy shape you'd see when a flag is blowing.

The shot above is created using a clever filter called Stamper that repeats the image as thumbnails and colours them to make up a larger version of the image.

There's even a Television filter that creates the effect you'd see when your TV was on the blink or had a badly tuned ariel. Why you'd want this I don't know!

And how about a Stain! make your pictures look as though you've spilled coffee on them. Comes complete with authentic edges, what next!

Xenofex's Fluffy clouds (above) is like the Photoshop Clouds filter but lays them over the image so it's much more practical.

The Lightning filter can be used to create realsitic streaks of lightning (left).

Corel have recently aquired the Ultimate program Knockout. It can be used as a stand alone program but is an excellent addition to your digital imaging collection, especially if you own an older version of Photoshop that doesn't have the extract mode. To use this you draw around the inner and outer edges of the area you want to select and let the program run. It then creates a cutout that's often near on perfect, even round hair.

The cutout can be exported which saves it as a TIFF with an Alpha channel. This can be opened in Photoshop and made into a selection.

This selection of squirrel would have been near on impossible using a standard selection tool. Here the cut out is stunningly accurate.

Appendix F: Plug-in filters

Continued.

Eye Candy is another plug in from Alien Skin with some superb effects. If you're interested in creating text, buttons and graphical treats for your Web pages, look no further than the Chrome filter. It produces stunning metallic effects and has a range of surfaces and bevels to give realism.

The image above was created using a simple shape made using the Selection tool and then Chrome filter with a bevel was applied. The same shape below has had the Glass filter applied which can be used to create great plastic or glass effects.

The shot above was generated using the Fur filter. The result seems to take ages to apply, but can be quite effective.

Eye Candy's Glass filter can be set to produce effects like you'd expect to see when looking at your subject through a glass window.

Eye Candy's Drip filter places droplets of water over the subject.

The Jiggle filter (above) distorts the image, the Fire filter adds...er...fire, and the Smoke filter...you guessed it!

The Marble filter (above) creates superb marble layers of the colours of your choice that can be used as backgrounds or as text and button fills. Weave (below) adds a weave pattern over the image.

Appendix G: Recording sheets

Use these to make notes of all your favourite filter settings.
Photocopy the sheets if you prefer not to mark this book.

UNSHARP MASK

Photograph	Size	Amount	Radius	Threshold
Blue racing car	1280x960	123%	1.4	103

GAUSSIAN BLUR

Photograph	Size	Radius	Fade	Mode
Portrait of Katie	1760x1200	7.3 pixels	70 %	Soft light

DUOTONES, TRITONES & QUADTONES

Photograph	Ink 1	Ink 2	Ink 3	Ink 4
Deeping village	Black	PANTONE 431 CVC	PANTONE 492 CVC	PANTONE 556 CVC

DROP SHADOW

Photograph	Mode	Color	Opacity	Angle	Global	Distance	Spread	Size	Noise
Web button	Multiply	Blue	7 5 %	1 2 0°	On	5px	7 %	8px	4 %

INNER & OUTER GLOW

Photograph	Mode	Color	Opacity	Noise	Technique	Spread	Size	Range	Jitter
Neon Text	Hard light	Green	75%	8 %	Softer	4 %	6px	50%	3 %

BEVEL & EMBOSS

Photo	Structure					Shading		Highlight			Shadow		
	Style	Tech	Depth	Size	Soft	Angle	Altitude	Mode	Color	Opac	Mode	Color	Opac
Pencils	Inn.B	Sm	100%	5px	1px	30°	25°	Screen	Black	23°	Inner	Blue	23%

LIGHTING EFFECTS

Photograph	Style	Light type	Intensity	Focus	Gloss	Material	Exposure
Stonehenge	Crossing D	Omni	35	-23	39	-32	-23

Ambience	Texture channel	Height
– 2 3	Red	8 8

HUE & SATURATION

Photograph	Hue	Saturation	Lightness
Robin	+ 2 7	– 1 3	–8

Also available from Focal Press ...

Adobe Photoshop 6.0 for Photographers
Martin Evening

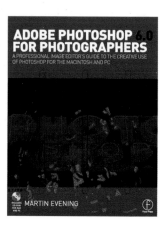

A professional image editor's guide to the creative use of Photoshop for the Macintosh and PC.

Adobe Photoshop 6.0 has become a classic reference source written to deal directly with the needs of photographers. Whether you are an accomplished user or are just starting out, this book contains a wealth of practical advice, hints and tips to help you achieve professional-looking results.

- Includes free CD-Rom with movie tutorials in Mac and PC format

I wish I had bought this book before spending a fortune on other much more expensive books. This book is written in terms that are easy and interesting to follow. I would certainly recommend it.
Amazon.co.uk reader

The book is very production-orientated and herein lies its strength... It's reassuring to be taught by someone with many miles of real output to his name.
MacUser

November 2000 • 448pp • colour throughout • 246 x 189mm • Paperback with CD-Rom
ISBN 0 240 51633 8

***To order your copy call +44 (0)1865 888180 (UK) or +1 800 366 2665 (USA)
or visit the Focal Press website***

---

www.focalpress.com
- The most comprehensive and up-to-date list of books on all aspects of media technology and practice
- Articles by industry experts on the latest techniques and technology
- The best industry job sites
- Information on major media events
- Training and support material for media courses
- A forum to discuss issues with fellow peers and leading professionals